HOW TO MAKE GOOD THINGS HAPPEN

HOW TO MAKE GOOD THINGS HAPPEN

Know Your Brain, Enhance Your Life

MARIAN ROJAS ESTAPÉ, MD

Translated from the Spanish by Sofia Smith-Laing

Countryman Press

An Imprint of W. W. Norton & Company
Independent Publishers Since 1923

Names and potentially identifying characteristics of the patients described in this book have been changed or omitted, and most patients are composites.

Countryman Press
www.countrymanpress.com

An imprint of W. W. Norton & Company, Inc.
500 Fifth Avenue, New York, NY 10110
www.wwnorton.com

978-1-68268-647-8 (pbk.)

10 9 8 7 6 5 4 3 2

To my six men

CONTENTS

THE START OF A JOURNEY

*A journey of a thousand miles begins with
a single step.*

—Laozi

Planes, trains, and other modes of transportation are generally excellent places for surprising things to happen. You just have to let yourself be carried along, observing and intervening if a good opportunity arises. My best stories have come out of such situations.

A few years ago, on a flight from New York to London, I was traveling in the window seat. I always choose this seat because I like watching the sky, the clouds, and the sea; above all, I like to remind myself of the insignificance of human beings in the face of nature's immensity, so as to gain some perspective about what happens to us on Earth.

I always pay attention to the traveler seated next to me. Over the long hours in flight, one develops a certain connection to one's neighbor. Analyzing what they're reading and what they watch on their screen, observing whether they eat or sleep—speculating about their circumstances and the reasons for their trip is unavoidable. Do they have a family? Are they traveling for work? At one moment or another, one of you gets up, and good manners require that you exchange a few simple words. Generally, at the end of the flight, you wish each other a friendly goodbye.

I've always believed that if you pay close enough attention to anyone, they become interesting. One usually has a conversation at some point during the flight. Thanks to these interactions, I've met truly fascinating people, and things have happened to me that have made an impact on many aspects of my life.

On this particular flight, taking off from New York, I sat next to an older gentleman. He was reading the newspaper, and I got some course notes out of my bag. They were on anatomy; the drawings I'd done in class weren't very good—I've always been bad at drawing—and while I was trying to memorize the hundreds of names, I noticed the man's gaze directed at my papers. I smiled at him.

"I study medicine."

He answered, "My father is a doctor."

I did a quick analysis of the man—I've loved doing this since I was young—but he maintained, despite our cordiality, a cold, unapproachable look. I grew curious, and asked, "Have you followed in your father's footsteps, professionally?"

"No. I've always preferred investigation."

"What kind?"

"I investigate terrorism."

I closed my notes. A conversation had fallen in my lap that promised to be very interesting. My collection of muscles and strange little bones would still be there when I got to Madrid. My interlocutor revealed to me that he had just retired after more than thirty years with the CIA. For a while now, he had been allowed to speak more freely of his work, and during the rest of the flight he explained the war in Iraq and geopolitical tensions in the area, conflicts over oil and pipelines, the interests of different Western countries . . . all of it on an improvised map of the Middle East with arrows pointing in every direction.

I'm a politics and history buff, and I have to confess that I didn't stop taking notes the whole time. At one point in the conversation, I told him

I was studying to be a psychiatrist. He scrutinized me and was silent for a few moments before beginning to ask me the strangest questions about my tastes and personality. I'm not used to being asked about myself with so much intensity, as it's usually me who's posing the questions, but I tried to respond as sincerely as possible.

After a pause, he proposed that I do a stint at the CIA when I had finished my specialized studies and undertake some kind of work as a forensic or investigative psychiatrist. In that moment my eyes lit up. The world suddenly seemed so exciting. I smiled and said, "As long as I don't have to do field work—I tend to be a little nervous."

He left me his contact details and we said goodbye. I wrote to him several times and we maintained an email correspondence for a few years.

Unfortunately, reader, I never did go and work at the CIA. My life took another course, but I keep that card from my "analyst friend" in my wallet, to remind myself that opportunities are close by—you just have to go look for them.

In my opinion, few notions have done more damage than the idea that "it will arrive when you least expect it." No one is going to come looking for us at home to offer us our life's work. We have to go out and find it.

One of the things in life that causes us the most anguish is the inability to know what we should devote ourselves to or what path we should choose. Making a decision becomes an impossible challenge. We live in a world full of opportunities—we have never had so much available for so little effort. We find ourselves living at the most overstimulated point in history; today, any seven-year-old has absorbed more information and stimuli—music, sound, food, flavors, images, videos—than any human being who previously walked the Earth.

This overstimulation makes decisions hard. Today's younger generations—the so-called "millennial" generation, where I have one foot planted, and "Gen Z"—find themselves bewildered, unsure what to choose or where to go. Professionally, they have to decide between innumerable fields of study, and, once their studies are complete, between innumerable job opportunities; both of these choices seem impossible. Multiple possibilities crowd in, and they don't know where to direct their lives. Ours is a society of confusion and commitment phobia. I see more and more young people who are "blocked" without knowing it, because to decide, one needs to know what one feels.

Millennials and members of Gen Z are saturated with emotions and feelings that make them reliant on constant gratification to move forward. We'll speak more about this later, and we will try to understand better what is happening in the minds of many young people. There is a clear breach between two generations who are living in the same world: those born before 1980 and those born after 1990. Those of us born between 1980 and 1990 have lived through an important period of transition.

Those born before 1980 have generally struggled quite a bit: many were born to the children of twentieth-century wars and have given their families a good start; most important of all, the digital world of the internet and social networks has caught up to them after adolescence. This is key. Their personal relationships, their ways of working and confronting life, as well as their beliefs, are all based on other concepts—I don't mean specific ideologies, I mean the way that they're formed.

After 1990, something decisive happens: the birth of the internet. In this book, we'll examine the impact of the constant assault of stimuli that the youngest members of our society are subjected to as soon as they're born, as well as the effect of social networks on the gratification system of the brain, which is the reason that we find ourselves dealing with a profoundly unsatisfied generation. To motivate them—in educational, emotional, affective, professional, and economic terms—more and more frequent and intense stimuli are often required.

How to Make Good Things Happen draws on many different tools. Life contains very difficult moments, when the most important thing is to survive and find some support to sustain oneself. The rest of the time, we need to fight to bring out our BPS—Best Possible Selves.* We'll talk about attitude and optimism; the way that we confront life has a big impact on what happens to us. Predisposition—the attitude we already have in place—determines how we respond to any situation.

Years of experiments have shown that the way you decide to respond to problems and questions encountered on a daily basis can influence the outcome. The brain, physiological markers, genes, cells, feelings, emotions, and thoughts function as a whole. Physical ailments, in many cases, have a direct relationship to the emotions, and we can always try to channel the effect that a physical ailment has on our state of mind. To help you understand the brain, I will attempt to simplify what is fundamentally complex. By understanding our brains and managing our emotions, we can enhance our lives. Nowadays, neuroscience, specifically neurobiology, taken together with what we call the unconscious—from surface emotions to the depths of the psyche—can explain a large part of our behavior.

This book talks about happiness, because we all long to find it, and about success. But success can be a great liar. In my therapeutic practice, I often find myself admiring people who, faced with suffering, pain, and failure, have been capable of overcoming them. Failure reveals what success conceals, says the great teacher of my life, my father.

In this book I want to try to explain not only the troubles of the mind, heart, and body, but, much more than that, the good and healthy aspects of life. I want to show what can help the reader to enjoy better health in soul and body, and in this way, perhaps, to get closer to that longed-for happiness.

This is the start of an exciting path toward understanding and reinventing ourselves. Everyone has a second chance to find their passion and to choose a better way through life.

---

* We'll look at this formula, BPS, in Chapter 9.

1

DESTINATION: HAPPINESS

Happiness can't be defined; it can only be experienced. You have to feel it to recognize it, and once you do, words seem to fall short of expressing it. All the same, we're going to try to explain it, approaching it from different angles.

The first idea I want to get across is this: there are no cheat sheets or shortcuts that guarantee happiness. There's already a lot of criticism out there of self-help books that promise a simple recipe to happiness, but what's true is that we now have a multitude of studies and scientific data that give us a fairly specific sense of the level of physical and psychological well-being indispensable to happiness.

Psychiatrists study mental illness—or rather, we study people who suffer from mental or emotional disturbances. Frequent professional conferences are held on the most varied issues in the field: the brain or some specific region of it, neuronal markers and the physiology behind them, internal or external factors that make psychiatric illness more likely; or how to improve the reliability of diagnostics, and the latest experimental treatments. In general, we look at mental afflictions through every possible scientific lens.

Since I was young, my vocation has been to treat and help people suffering from sadness and anguish. This has led me to investigate happiness, pleasure, love, compassion, and joy and to pose myself a series of difficult questions. Why are there people with a tendency to suffer and complain, no matter their situation? Does good luck exist or is it not as random as it seems? What importance do genes carry in forming people's minds and their characters? Which factors predispose me to be—or prevent me from being—happier? Investigating these issues has pushed me down lots of different paths, in search of the most thought-provoking reading.

Our society is, at present, richer than ever in comparative terms. We have never had as much as we do now. Generally, our primary needs are taken care of and we have almost any item at our disposal, in most cases only a click away. As a consequence, though it isn't desirable and should be avoided, overabundance is becoming normal.

Sometimes we believe that we deserve everything, an attitude encouraged by our reigning materialism, which makes us think that it's good to have access to everything that we desire. However, no accumulation of things on its own can grant access to happiness, to an *interior* state of plenitude.

Happiness consists in having a fully realized life, in which we try to get the best out of our values and aptitudes. Happiness is making a little work of art out of life, striving every day to bring out our best selves.

> *Happiness is intimately related to the meaning*
> *we give our lives and our existence.*

As we will see, the first step toward trying to be happy is recognizing what we are asking for from life. In a world that has lost its meaning and its sense of direction, we tend to substitute "sensations" for that "sense." Society is suffering from a huge spiritual vacuum that it tries to fill with a frantic search for sensations: bodily satisfaction, sex, food, alcohol, etc. There is a widespread and insatiable need to experience new and ever more intense emotions and sensations. There is nothing bad *per se* about sex, gourmet cooking, or the pleasure of a glass of good wine—I'm talking about when the search for these sensations is substituted for true meaning in life. In these cases, where the sense of direction has been lost, the accumulation of sensations produces a momentary gratification; meanwhile, our interior void grows like a black hole, slowly engulfing our lives, inevitably leading to psychological ruptures or destructive behaviors.

Only then, when the damage is done, does the affected person, or someone close to them, realize that recovery is beyond their own strength and seek external help. This is when someone in the role of a psychiatrist or psychologist becomes necessary to help rebuild a person's life.

Human beings seek to possess, and we connect happiness with possession. We spend our lives seeking economic, social, professional, and affective stability. We seek security, prestige, material things, friends. But true happiness is not in *having*, it is in *being*. Our way of being is the foundation of true happiness.

> *Careful! Take care not to confuse happiness with happiness lite, which is sold to us as though it were only a click away. You know there's something wrong with this materialist concept when 20 percent of the population is seeking treatment for emotional problems.*

If amassing material things isn't the solution to happiness, what is? In my opinion, in this constantly changing and rapidly evolving world, happiness must necessarily involve a return to values. And what are values? Values help us to be better people, to perfect ourselves. It's a very basic definition, but it serves as a guide in moments of chaos and uncertainty.

When someone loses themself and doesn't know where to go, having values and a few guiding principles helps stop the boat from running aground. Aristotle said it long ago, in his *Nicomachean Ethics*: "Shall we not, like archers who have a mark to aim at, be more likely to hit upon what is right?" Today there are no marks to aim at, the archers have died out, and arrows are flying randomly in all directions.

To understand the world we're facing, I find this acronym from the US Army War College helpful: VUCA. It's a phrase that really nails our sociological context: volatility, uncertainty, complexity, and ambiguity. This notion was formed to describe the state of the world in the aftermath of the Cold War. Now it's used in leadership strategy, sociological analysis, and education to describe sociocultural, psychological, and political conditions.

Volatility refers to rapidity of change. Nothing seems stable: online news portals update every few seconds to suck in readers, trends in what to wear and where to be seen can change in a matter of days, and the economy and stock exchanges fluctuate hour by hour.

Uncertainty: few things are predictable. Events follow one after the other, and we feel flattened by a whirlwind of fresh occurrences. There are algorithms that try to foresee the future, but reality ends up surpassing fiction.

Complexity refers to the interconnectedness of our world, where all areas of human knowledge have reached an infinitesimal level of precision. Even the smallest details influence outcomes in our lives—the famous "Butterfly Theory" of chaos.

Ambiguity—which, for me, has a connection to relativism—leaves no room for clarity in our ideas. Everything might or might not be. There are no clear ideas left about almost any aspect of existence.

I've always thought that psychiatry is a marvelous profession. It is the science of the soul. We help people who come to us asking for help in understanding how their minds, their information-processing systems, their emotions, and their behaviors work. We try to heal past wounds or teach them to manage situations that are difficult or impossible to control. There are plenty of books out there now to teach you to find your focus in life or deal with different aspects of it. Like everything, you need to know how to filter through these, and above all, how to find the way of dealing with things that suits you best. We psychiatrists and psychologists must adapt ourselves to our patients, understanding their silences, their difficult moments, their fears, and their worries, all while providing order and calm without judgment and knowing how to communicate serenity and optimism.

I find it fascinating to look into how we think, why we react the way we do, what emotions are, and how they're reflected in the mind. Ultimately, happiness has a lot to do with the way in which I observe, analyze, and judge myself, and with my expectations for myself and my life. Put simply, happiness is to be found in balancing my personal, relational, and professional aspirations with what I have actually achieved, piece by piece. Finding this balance has results: adequate self-esteem and a fair evaluation of my worth.

CASE STUDY: MAMEN

Mamen is a 33-year-old patient. She works as an administrator in a large company. She lives with her parents, with whom she has a good relationship. She has a boyfriend, a shy and withdrawn guy who cares for her very attentively. There's a good atmosphere at her work and sometimes she meets up with people from the office.

One day she comes to my practice. She says her self-esteem is through the floor. She can't explain why, and adds: "My parents love me, I like my job, I have friends, but I feel like a waste of space."

After giving me a summary of her life, she stops short and tells me, "I'm ashamed to be here, telling my problems to a stranger when I have nothing to complain about." She gets up, heads for the door, and leaves. I go after her and tell her to come back, that we had better finish the session because, if she is sad or upset, it's because something isn't working internally. In the end she calms down and agrees to come back.

She's been in therapy for eight months. She is much better, but I know that every day in the middle of consultation she'll have what I call "one of her moments." She gets overwhelmed and confesses, "I'm ashamed to be here, I'm telling my life to a stranger."

And she tries to leave. It's a struggle for her to accept that she is sharing her life with another person. Little by little she's understanding and articulating the reasons she needs to resolve those internal conflicts that are preventing her from growing.

I could always say to a person acting like this, "No need to come back, when you feel comfortable call and make an appointment."

But I accept her experience in the moment and continue the counseling session without judgment, as though she hasn't said anything.

SELF-ESTEEM AND HAPPINESS

Self-esteem and happiness are intimately related. A person at peace with themselves, who maintains a certain internal equilibrium and takes pleasure in the little things in life, will normally have an adequate level of self-esteem.

NO SELF-ESTEEM PROBLEMS HERE

Miguel de Unamuno was one of the best authors of the great Spanish "generation of 98." He was well known for his earthy, familiar personality. On one occasion he was honored with the Grand Cross of Alfonso X the Wise, given to him by King Alfonso XIII himself.

Unamuno, known for being a militant republican and a member of the Socialist Party, at the moment the award was being conferred, remarked, "I am honored, majesty, to receive this cross that I so richly deserve."

The king, surprised but familiar with the writer's reputation, replied, "How curious! In general, most of those honored insist that they don't deserve the cross."

Unamuno, with his habitual familiarity, responded with a smile, "Sir, in those cases it was true—*they* did not deserve it."

HAPPINESS AND SUFFERING

They say you don't know what happiness is until you've lost it. When confronted with pain, suffering, grief, or financial problems, an inner voice says, "I'm not happy! This is hell! Why do I have such bad luck?" At those times we find it difficult to look back at happy moments we have had or to appreciate the glimmers of joy that filled us at other times.

Life is a constant beginning again, a path where we walk through joyful occurrences or moments of happiness, but also hard times. To be happy we must be capable of rebuilding ourselves as much as possible in the face of trauma and hardship. The reason is simple: there is no life story without its wounds. Failures, and how one frames them, are the most decisive aspect of anyone's trajectory in life. We as human beings, over the whole course of our lives, pass through very demanding and difficult moments, which mean that we will not be able to be happy if we do not learn to get over them, or at least try.

As a psychiatrist, in consultation, I've treated every kind of trauma, and I am conscious in writing these lines that very difficult life stories exist, some much more than others. There are things beyond our control that we cannot change. We cannot choose a lot of what will happen to us in life, but we are absolutely free, each and every one of us, to choose the attitude with which we confront it. We are dealt some cards, good or bad, but they're the ones we have and we must play them as well as we can.

Man needs tools to overcome the wounds and traumas of the past. The periods that demolish us physically and psychologically leave important traces on our life stories. The ways in which we as individuals overcome and start again mark many aspects of our personalities. This talent is born from an inner strength that we all have, though it may be developed to a greater or lesser degree: resilience.

The concept of resilience was made fashionable by the French doctor Boris Cyrulnik. This psychiatrist, the son of Jewish immigrants from the Ukraine, was born in Bordeaux in 1937. Under the Nazi occupation, when he was only five years old, his parents were arrested and deported to concentration camps, but he fled, hid in a series of locations, and finally was taken in at a farm, living under the false identity of a non-Jewish boy called Jean Laborde. The war over, his foster family encouraged him to study medicine and become a psychiatrist.

Young Boris soon realized that, through his own life story, he could understand the causes of trauma and try to help others—for the most part, children—to rebuild themselves after a trauma or an emotional rupture.

The Oxford English Dictionary defines resilience as "the ability of a substance to return to its original shape after it has been bent, stretched or pressed." Cyrulnik expanded the meaning of the concept to include "the capacity of a human being to recover from a trauma and, without being marked for life, to be happy."

Resilience sends us a message of hope. It used to be thought that traumas suffered in infancy were impossible to erase, and endured, leaving a decisive mark on the trajectory of the affected child's life. How can we overcome such deep and painful wounds? The key lies in solidarity, love, and contact with others; in essence, the key is warmth.

Cyrulnik, over the course of his long experience, shows many examples of this. At the University of Toulon, where he is a professor, he works with Alzheimer's sufferers. Many of them have forgotten words, but not attachments, music, gestures, or demonstrations of affection. Cyrulnik insists on the flexibility of the psyche. Before, it was thought that a person was permanently marked by pain and suffering. If a person overcomes their trauma, their wound, they become someone resilient.

In helping them to overcome, it is key not to blame someone for their past errors, and to give them support and affection. There are multiple therapies for this. A few years ago I worked in Cambodia freeing girls from child prostitution. It was unequivocally one of the periods of my life that has most marked me.

I devoted myself to visiting the brothels of Cambodia and rescuing girls in deplorable conditions. I remember with crystal clarity one girl, aged 13 and recently rescued from a prostitution network, who asked me with a hopeless look, "Will I ever be able to have a normal life—to enjoy anything?"

The message of hope is there, science explains it, and my experience has taught it to me. There are methods for curing the deepest wounds. Over the course of these pages, I'll tell you how I ended up collaborating on this passion project in Cambodia and some of the other stories that have marked my life. Every step on the path I've traveled has helped me to understand the human brain better. Along with it, I have understood suffering better too, and, ultimately, the road to happiness.

TRAUMA

A traumatic event destroys one's identity and one's convictions, about others and about the world. This rupture is the beginning of what we know as trauma. Cyrulnik has established that in order for us to suffer a trauma, we must undergo what is known as a double blow. The first blow is the perturbing event itself, the traumatic occurrence proper; but for this to take root in a person's life, a second blow must occur, dependent on the behavior of those around them. In broad strokes, the second blow is an implication of rejection or abandonment, stigmatization, disgust, contempt, or humiliation, with incomprehension being a quality common to all of these.

According to Boris Cyrulnik, these are the three pillars of resilience:

- Personal. Having internal tools to rely on from birth; secure attachment. This is one of the strongest means there is overcome a trauma.
- Social and familial context. The kind of support delivered by carers, parents, and other close figures. These are key for pulling through after a painful trauma (this is where the second blow really comes into play).

- Societal context. That is to say, being able to rely on social and legal support at such times—the support of the community—mitigates the trauma and strengthens the victim.

> *Cyrulnik: "Imagine a child has had a problem,*
> *that he has received a blow, and when he tells*
> *his parents about the problem, they let slip a*
> *movement of disgust, a reproach. In that moment,*
> *they have transformed his suffering into trauma."*

CASE STUDY: LUCÍA

Lucía is a six-year-old girl. She lives with her parents and her two brothers, who are seven and two. She goes to the school in her neighborhood and is a very happy, creative girl with a huge imaginative capacity.

One day, at a birthday party at the house of one of her school friends, she goes into the bathroom. When she goes in, she sees that the father of a boy in her class is already in there. She steps back out and politely apologizes. The man in question—he doesn't deserve a name—tells her in a friendly way to come in. He drops his trousers and asks Lucía to touch him.

The little girl, frightened, obeys. The next thing he does is take off her under-wear and put his hand under her dress.[*] Paralyzed, Lucía can't speak or cry out.

The man threatens the little girl, telling her she mustn't tell anyone anything, or he'll hurt her and her brothers. Lucía leaves the bathroom and hides in a cor-ner to cry. Her parents aren't at the party, but she hopes they get there as soon as possible.

Half an hour later, she sees them come into the house. She observes the man from the bathroom approach them and greet them amicably, saying that their daughter has behaved very well and is very polite. Lucía starts to sweat and wants to cry. The man approaches her, takes her by the hand, and says: "Your parents are

---

* I will refrain from giving further details that might trigger the reader's sensitivities.

here, and I've already told them that you behaved very well. Give your brothers a kiss when you see them."

Lucía is sure of herself, and, once they get in the car, the first thing she does is tell her parents what happened. They don't believe it, but they listen to her with absolute attention. After a couple of days, they come to my practice to ask advice and see how to deal with it. They're not sure that it's true, but whatever the case, they don't want to hurt their daughter any further.

I treated Lucía for half a year. She had nightmares, she was afraid of dealing with older men, she felt sad, and she didn't want to go to school.

From the first moment, her parents showed her their support. The matter was brought to court; Lucía learned to develop her inner strength; today she is a healthy and happy girl of 13. A few months ago, she came to see me at my practice to tell me that she's going to Ireland for a term to learn English. Her words of farewell were: "I'm not afraid anymore, I've overcome it. I want to thank you for supporting me, for believing me, and for strengthening my relationship with my parents. I know they doubted me for a little while; the fact that they supported me to the end and that you treated me from the start has freed me from a huge trauma for good."

Being happy means being capable of overcoming setbacks and getting up again after.

The present moment can at times become a nightmare. Sometimes one longs to flee into the future. At other times one gets blocked and remains paralyzed inside a particular memory or a past traumatic event. Getting stuck in the past turns us into bitter, rancorous people, incapable of forgetting the damage done or emotional suffering.

We have all passed through stages when we realize we need a pause or a break in order to regather our strength after a physically or psychologically demanding period, or simply in order to get ready to try again for a goal that we have yet to achieve. During such a lull, above all at the start of a holiday, exhaustion and tension tend to crop up. We feel more vulnerable than ever. This vulnerability is more than just psychic; relaxing the body after a period of exertion produces a general lowering of our defenses, which makes it likelier we will contract colds, flu, or other sicknesses.

It is precisely those post-tension moments that are the most important to our psychological trajectory, given that the way we confront them dictates whether we can overcome major mental upsets. We must be vigilant in these seasons because frequently it is only when we slow our activity and have more time, when we stop to think, that we can tell whether our psychological health is at risk from anything that has happened. In any case, battles are won by tired soldiers, wars by the masters of inner strength. This inner strength will help us to overcome our problems. We cultivate it by learning to dominate the inner "I," those thoughts of the past or worries for the future that torment us and stop us from living in a balanced way in the present.

Time does not heal all wounds, but it does shift what is most painful away from the direct gaze. Suffering is therefore the school where we learn strength. When the torrent that rushes out of suffering is accepted in a "healthy" way, one gains an important form of self-control fundamental to life.

Balance means learning to maintain a certain inner peace, equanimity, and harmony despite the thousands of challenges life throws at us.

After the blow, one must take back the reins of one's own life in order to achieve the life purpose that one has decided on. We must be masters of our own destinies. The simplest thing is to think short-term, to live according to our reactions to the anarchic external impulses that affect us, letting ourselves be carried along; what is better, although more difficult to achieve, is to design one's life with long-term objectives, so that, even if something turns us out of our path, we can reorient ourselves toward our goals. A person without a project, who doesn't know what they want to become, and who doesn't find meaning in their life, cannot be happy.

The solution does not lie in pills. Medication is key for moments of blockage when the organism itself is incapable of recuperating on its own, or when circumstances are so adverse that we require an extra support in order not to collapse. Medication regulates elevated or depleted chemicals in the brain. It does not replace cerebral or mental functions, but it allows you to feel or accomplish these functions when they aren't working.

Medication can offer solutions, but there is another effective and helpful therapy: the doctor's bedside manner. A few encouraging words and true, engaged listening can have a significant healing effect.

BEDSIDE MANNER IS THE BEST PAINKILLER

An article published in *The Journal of Pain* in May 2017 discussed the importance of the doctor's attitude in consultation. It has been demonstrated that, if a patient has confidence in their doctor, their sensation of pain diminishes. The doctor herself acts as a placebo. For example, what happens if the doctor vacations in the same place as a patient, or has similar tastes? Elizabeth Losin, a researcher working on the University of Miami study, observed that a feeling of social, educational, cultural, or religious connection helped lower patients' pain levels. If someone visiting a doctor feels sure that their pain is going to be lessened, this feeling of confidence has a positive effect. The brain, presented with the mere hope of relief, releases chemical substances from the endorphin family that assuage pain.

It very often happens that when someone visits a trusted doctor, a long-standing therapist, or a specialist in their particular ailment, after explaining what's bothering them, they notice an automatic improvement in their symptoms.

A doctor should be a "human vitamin" for their patients. In a world like today's, with its overextended health service, this is not easy. There isn't the time. It is often simpler, more practical, and more efficient to cure symptoms with pills. But sometimes a smile, a positive remark, or a hopeful phrase is enough to halt the development of a disease.

SUFFERING HAS MEANING

Contemporary society flees from suffering, and when we come across it certain questions arise: Do I deserve it? Is this happening because of my past mistakes? Why has God allowed this to happen? Let's consider some potentially helpful aspects of suffering.

Pain Possesses a Human and Spiritual Value

It can lift us to a higher plane and make us better people. How many people have you met who have been capable, after a blow, of getting back up and finding new ways forward in their lives, even expressing gratitude after the fact? It isn't rare to meet people who, after carrying on a superficial and conformist existence, have been transformed by suffering a difficult setback.

Suffering Helps Us to Reflect

It takes us to the heart of many questions that we might otherwise never have asked ourselves. Pain, when it arises, pushes us to clarify the meanings of our lives and of our deepest convictions. Masks and appearances fall away, and our real selves emerge.

Pain Helps Us to Accept Our Own Limitations

We become more vulnerable beings and come down from the pedestal that we or others have set ourselves on. At such times we must lower our gazes and recognize that we need help and the affection and support of others. On our own, we are not enough. Sharing our limitations with others can be the first step toward simplicity and overcoming the calamities we've suffered. The consciousness of our limitations reinforces our solidarity with others, our empathy with their pain, and, ultimately, our love for them.

Suffering Transforms the Heart

After a difficult period in which pain plays a leading role, one gets closer to other people's souls. We become capable of empathizing and of better understanding those around us. When someone feels loved, their life changes—they become illuminated and transmit that light in their turn. Authentic love is strengthened by pain when it is accepted in a healthy way that frees us from egotism. Anyone who expands their capacity for empathy is more lovable—they let themselves be loved—and turns their environment into a more welcoming place to live.

Suffering Can Be the Pathway to Happiness

We all have the will to achieve happiness and possess the tools to do so. Pain leads to a true maturing of the personality, more care for others, and a better knowledge of oneself.

> *There is only one antidote to suffering,*
> *pain, and sickness: love.*

Let's turn now to look underneath the surfaces of ourselves as human beings to understand the thoughts and emotions that hinder us and how our brains respond to stress or conflict. Simplicity takes a long time to achieve. Let us begin.

2

THE ANTIDOTE TO SUFFERING: LOVE

In this chapter I divide love into five chief types:

- Healthy love for oneself: self-esteem[*]
- Love for another person
- Love for others
- Love of ideals and beliefs
- Love of memories

LOVE FOR ANOTHER PERSON

> *There is no man so cowardly that love cannot transform him into a valiant hero.*
>
> —Plato

---

[*] See Chapter 1.

Falling in love is the greatest thing there is. Everything changes when you give your heart away to someone else! Everyone holds marvels and treasures in the depths of their being, which are revealed by real love. There is no human being that love cannot turn into someone more passionate and full of life. Human beings need to love. Love is the great matter of life.

Falling in love marks a person forever, and
life's most intense feelings come from love.

The aim of this book is not to discuss love between couples, but how healthy romantic love affects all aspects of life positively.

LOVE FOR OTHERS

Acting in solidarity and doing charitable work—in order to give oneself to others—have a protective effect on the mind and body. Feeling loved and not feeling alone are among the keys to happiness. In this life, the majority of our relationships, agreements, exchanges, and moments of enjoyment and pleasure are related to our interactions with others. For a romantic relationship to work well, or a negotiation, a business, a family—whether blood relations or ones by marriage—it is fundamental that relations between the people involved are easy, or at least relatively healthy.

On occasion, certain people around you will rub you the wrong way, and their mere presence will unsettle you. If you don't change something, they risk becoming toxic elements in your life. If living or working with certain people constantly gives you the sense of being in a hostile, tense atmosphere that keeps you on the alert, you may eventually get sick or mired in deep suffering. These people are "emotional vampires," at least for you, because they drag you down emotionally. We instinctively tend to cultivate connections and friendships with people who are positive and healthy to relate to, as much in our social lives as in a familial or professional context. We push away hostile, negative people, whose contributions always feel poisonous.

Robert Waldinger is an American psychiatrist in charge of the best study yet made of happiness. It consists of a long-term experiment that is still relevant today. The study began by examining the lives of two groups of men: a first group who were, in 1938, second-year students at Harvard, and a second group of boys from the poorest, most marginalized neighborhoods in Boston. The objective was to study these people's lives from adolescence through to adulthood, with the goal of determining what made them happy. Over the course of 75 years, the subjects of the experiment were asked questions about their work, their family life, and their health. Today, 60 of the 724 men who began the experiment are still participating in it—most of them by now are 90 or older—and they are currently beginning to study the more than 2,000 children the subjects fathered.

At the beginning of the study, these young people were interviewed just as their fathers had been. They underwent medical examinations, family reunions were held, their clinical histories were followed, their blood analyzed, their brains scanned.... What conclusions were drawn from the experiment? Researchers were surprised by the results. They held no lessons about wealth, fame, or the importance of working particularly hard, or even about the physiological and medical aspects of life. The message was clear and simple: good relationships make us happier and healthier.

Thanks to this study, we have learned three things about human relations:

- Social connections benefit us, and loneliness kills. Baldly stated, it looks extreme, but it's true: loneliness kills. People who have more bonds with family, friends, or a wider community are happier, healthier, and live longer than people with fewer relationships. Loneliness has been shown to be profoundly toxic. People who live in isolation are statistically more likely to be unhappy and more susceptible to a decline in health during middle age; their cerebral function is more prone to swift decay in old age; and they die sooner. It's a serious and urgent issue, which we ought to deal with, given that in our society, a solitary existence is becoming more and more common. In 2017, studies were carried out that linked loneliness to Alzheimer's disease and other forms of dementia.

- The important thing is not the number of social bonds, but their quality, and the more intimate they are, the more important their quality becomes. Living in a constant state of conflict is harmful to the health. Marriages with high levels of conflict, or lacking in affection, are very detrimental. On the other hand, living with warm and healthy relationships affords us protections. In the study, cholesterol levels weren't found to predict how the subjects would age—their relationship satisfaction levels were. Those who felt the most satisfied at the age of 50 were also the healthiest at the age of 80.

- Good relationships don't just protect the body—they also protect the brain. We might have guessed this, but the study proved it. Having a secure attachment to someone else during old age affords protection, and these people's memories remained clearer for longer. Conversely, those people caught in relationships where they didn't feel they could rely on the other person lost their memories earlier.

What Are the Foundations of Good Relationships?

I would say that the foundation of any affective, social, or emotional bond—professional, friendly, or romantic—depends on the ability to have a proper relationship with others; that is to say, to connect in a way sufficient to generate a friendly atmosphere.

They say you don't get a second chance to make a first impression. Unless they really have to, nobody buys anything from a person they don't like or find off-putting. I've treated a few bankers in my practice, and I always think that it's impossible for anyone to let someone manage their money or their inheritance if there isn't a cordial relationship or even an affinity between them; similarly, all things being equal, we will buy a car or other goods from the person who has treated us best—unless the price is unbeatable.

Friendship is the highest form of interaction with others, after love. For a true friendship to arise, there must be harmony, an exchange of experiences and emotions. Friendship is formed of confidences and it breaks up over indiscretions. It must be carefully nurtured. Friendship consists of an equal relationship that contains intimacy and learning, which is why we need to work at it with persistence and attention to detail.

How Do We Build Proper Relationships with Others?

Here I bring together a few little ideas to guide us. You don't have to follow the suggestions below to the letter, but they can be very helpful. You can also use them as a way to test yourself and understand why there have been times in your life when negotiations, friendships, or family relationships broke down.

1. Take an interest in people

   I know a lot of people who tell me: "I just don't like people."

   This statement shocks me, because our best memories, in general, are of times spent with others, and one of the greatest satisfactions life holds is rooted in relating to others and feeling loved. I particularly remember a stand-offish friend of mine, taciturn but warm-hearted, telling me: "I can't stand most people."

   His job was one where success and remuneration depended on forming adequate connections with people. When I asked him how he got through the day—we were close enough that I could be frank with him—he answered: "My clients interest me."

   If you show up to a family reunion with cousins, aunts and uncles, or in-laws, the best way to connect is to take an interest in them, their lives, their work, and their health. But it has to be real, not for show. Don't give the impression of quizzing or investigating them—just approach them in a sincere and amiable way. Always make an effort to interest yourself in other people's lives.

2. Try to remember important information

Not everyone is lucky enough to be able to rely on a good memory for names and dates. Those people who successfully remember information about others, however, create much stronger bonds in a shorter time. If you bump into someone after not seeing them for a while, and you remember their wife's name or that their father was undergoing treatment for an illness, you automatically generate an agreeable sense of closeness. We all like for people to remember things about us without prying, but it takes an effort to achieve this.

David Rockefeller—of Chase Manhattan Bank—had a private index filled with more than 100,000 names, where he kept information about the encounters he had had with those individuals. This information helped him to create a sense of familiarity and make everyone he came across feel important and special.

My father has the habit of noting down everything about the people he knows. A while ago, while I was looking for the number of a restaurant in his phone, I came across this information:

> Pepe, the proprietor; married to Ana. They have three chil-
> dren; the youngest son worries them because he didn't fin-
> ish his studies. His father passed away a few months ago of
> Alzheimer's. Paco, the head waiter, has always worked there
> and has arthritis.

I was impressed, and I know that if he went into the restaurant, calling everyone by their names and asking them about their concerns, he would be able to quickly connect with everyone. I must emphasize that this quality requires effort, either by strengthening your hippocampus—the brain's memory center—or getting into the habit of keeping track of information such as birthdays, anniversaries, or the concerns of those around you in a notebook or diary.

3. **Deepen your knowledge of people's lives, interests, and professions**

This is especially important in the world of work. You must remember that the majority of agreements are made between people who have formed bonds of cordiality and friendliness. If you have a meeting with the director of your company, try to find something out about him or her. If you want to surprise your friends, do your research. If you want to bring joy into the life of a family member, involve yourself in what interests them. This requires time and willpower. Call your family and friends so as not to lose touch. A small effort produces huge results. Personalize things. Look for what each individual enjoys. Don't use the same speeches or messages with everyone around you. This obliges you to pay more attention to the details. If you need to get a present, look for something special—not necessarily expensive or costly, but simply something that shows you made the rounds to find the most intimate or personalized gift.

4. **Avoid judgment**

Everyone is different. We tend to judge, analyze, and pigeonhole people as soon as we meet them. This can be a defense mechanism or simply an automatic mental process designed to avoid internal change. Very critical people may experience a constant need to feel superior, or, on the other hand, may have a problem with insecurity and a lack of self-esteem.

To judge fairly, we must be very empathetic and have at our disposal a lot of information that we don't usually hold. Whatever the case, it is always wiser to remain silent. Silence is the gatekeeper of intimacy.

One must accept others as they are, even if they're different and what we see of them doesn't fit with our ideas. This doesn't mean that we should ignore reality—there *are* people who do wrong, or that we should distance ourselves from because they're toxic—but regarding most people, the healthiest thing is to keep a pluralistic, generous frame of mind and be open to admitting that there are people who don't conform to our criteria at all. Closing oneself off harshly to everything different should be avoided. If you only accept people who have a certain level of education or come from a certain class within society, if you're obsessed with fans of a certain football team or members of a certain trade or profession, if you systematically reject everyone who comes from a certain region, country, or continent—without a doubt your capacity to understand the world and those around you will be reduced and you'll lose out on many of the subtle nuances that make our world so rich and diverse. It's no good generalizing and rejecting social groups or particular categories of people. Everyone has something to offer us.

In my practice, I'm often surprised by what leaves me shaken or perturbed. In spite of my more than ten years of experience listening to stories of broken lives, from people who have suffered deep wounds, I still feel twinges of disquiet when certain experiences are related to me.

Doctors must be wary of countertransference; that is to say, what we feel towards patients, the ensemble of emotions, thoughts, and attitudes that come up for us in reaction to their stories. It's inevitable that certain individuals, whether because of their life stories, their ways of being, or their actions, provoke an initial sensation of recoil in me. It might be due to how they tell me about their trauma or suffering, or because their story triggers my own vulnerability, or simply because their way of behaving runs counter to my ethical principles.

SOMETIMES YOU CAN'T HELP JUDGING . . .

I remember a patient I was seeing a few years ago, an anxious and very sensitive man who was very much in love with his wife. He worked in a company's IT department, and his wife was a journalist. He was always worrying that she was unfaithful to him, largely because she traveled a lot internationally and had a life rich in friendships and social networks. She denied any kind of infidelity, but even so, he suffered greatly from this fear.

After three or four sessions, I asked the wife to come to my office. She came in, greeted me coldly, and almost before she sat down, said to me:

"You're obliged to keep client confidentiality, so you can't say anything to my husband. Of course I'm unfaithful to him, I have been ever since we started dating, but he'll never find out. Is there anything else?"

I have to confess that a chill ran down my spine. All the same, I tried to create a cordial atmosphere in the consulting room. It wasn't possible—in the face of this revelation, made with such determination and sense of impunity, I was blocked. She insisted that she enjoyed the adrenaline rush of cheating and having a double life, that she had always been that way and didn't want to change.

After listening to her life story for a while, I explained to her gently but firmly the reason why she was playing with her husband's feelings. She didn't care. Displaying the same coldness with which she had entered my consulting room, she left without saying goodbye. I continued to see the husband for a time, but they moved to another city and I didn't follow up with them. I don't think their future was rosy.

5. Don't impose your views, beliefs, or values

Work on being a role model for your children, employees, or friends. If you try to impose your views, you'll be met with rejection. Nowadays we know that demanding parents who impose their will without moderation on their offspring end up with erratic, rebellious children who are always looking to contradict them. Limits are necessary, and it's essential that people respect our ideas and beliefs, but we mustn't stray into severity or aggression. Society doesn't need masters, but instead, leaders. A leader sets an example for living, blending integrity, solid values, and modernity with the knowledge that they're an authentic and rational person.

If you want to influence someone or communicate your ideals, learn to be a good example.

It's one thing to impose your ideas, and another to ask that they be respected. There is no good leader who is not a good person. Today, the politics of many nations are full of talk of supposed leaders who really aren't; they're given that label in the media, but often when their private lives are revealed, it becomes clear that it was all a façade, just an appearance, and their conduct is directed by consultants and designed to create a good image—one that doesn't match up with reality. A good person is authentic. And authenticity is a matter of balance, where theory and practice must have a healthy relationship. We are what we do, not what we say. Actions speak louder than words. In this matter, the facts speak for themselves.

6. ### Surprise yourself by making the most of shared interests
    Friendship and good relationships arise where there are interests, values, and tastes in common. Look for these; it's rare that you have nothing in common with someone, even the most random person in your life, from your child's pediatrician to your financial adviser or the handyman who helps you out with odd jobs. You'll find, even if you aren't expecting it, that when you spend time on inner things—not just external, practical needs—you're taking an important step forward in your life. You see further, and your heart isn't just focused on the superficial aspects of relationships—getting advan-

tages or instant gratification out of people—but on what's inside them. Your relationships will be more honest and your inner growth will be exponential.

THE PIMPS AND BROTHELS OF CAMBODIA

When I arrived in Cambodia, I realized that accessing brothels in order to give therapy, or any other kind of help, as I hoped to do, would be complicated. The "hustlers" put all kinds of obstacles in our way. They demanded certain conditions and, for there to be any benefit in going into the brothels and speaking to the prostitutes, the procurers had to be cooperative.

I needed to find something in common with them, but it wasn't easy. Over the course of my life, however, I've come to realize through trial and error that there's one thing very few people will turn down: a Starburst. You might be laughing, but I go through a bowlful a day at my practice. Patients tell me that they're taking them for their children or grandchildren, but deep down I know that's not true. The candy is for them. Pineapple flavored Starbursts are particularly sought after. I've asked the company to send me bags of pineapple ones, but so far I haven't been successful.

I arrived in Cambodia with ten kilos of Starburst. After two weeks I had none left, but I found a perfect local copy. At the door of a brothel, accompanied by two nurses, with complete seriousness, I would say to the pimp in Khmer:

"Nek chom ñam skor krob te?"—that's how I pronounced it, anyway, and I was told that it meant, *Do you want a candy?*

Nobody ever said no. The guy in front of me, who gave off the worst impression, with a dirty, unscrupulous look, would sketch out a smile and nod his head yes. This infinitesimal little detail opened up the possibility of my entering their space in a warmer, less hostile way.

During the final weeks of my time there, the girls called me Madame Bonbon, which gave me a feeling of enormous tenderness.

7. Smile and laugh with people

If there isn't an easy way to connect, use a touch of humor. Very few people turn down a smile if it comes their way. Laughter is the shortest distance between two people, and, at the same time, it's one of the most efficient methods for increasing endorphin levels in the blood. Alice Isen, of Stanford University, conducted an important study on how expansive emotions—smiling, laughter, the pleasure of humor—markedly improve cognitive abilities and social conduct. She observed that these things all improve our creativity, organization, and planning and problem-solving abilities. This is due to the fact that laughter activates the flow of blood to the prefrontal cortex, the area in charge of these functions.

In another interesting study carried out in Bonn, Germany, it was observed that happy, joyful people show greater productivity and better performance at work.

Laughter and smiling have the capacity to alter the chemistry of our bloodstream, protecting us from certain illnesses and infections.

8. Sing, especially in a group

Singing in a group is beneficial to mental health. Recently a study was published in the journal *Medical Humanities* on how the act of singing in public can have a beneficial effect on mental health.

The authors—from the University of East Anglia—participated in a project called Sing Your Heart Out, in which they organized singing workshops every week and focused on at-risk members of the population as well as the general public. Some 120 people participated in the activity, of whom 80 had visited a mental health service. The groups were evaluated at various points over a six-month period.

Observation showed that singing and socializing have a striking effect on well-being, the improvement of social skills, and a sense of belonging. This is a clear demonstration of what Robert Waldinger describes in his research.

The strange thing is that while singing on your own—like we all do in the shower!—has always been a strong motivational tool, the act of singing in public has different and very positive effects for a sector of the population. Participants called the project a "lifesaver."

This brings to mind the case of the orchestra conductor Íñigo Pirfano. Now approaching 50, he is the founder of A Kiss for All the World. With his organization, he visits very tough places—prisons, hospitals, refugee camps, extremely poor areas—and conducts performances of Beethoven's Symphony No. 9, inspired by Schiller's *Ode to Joy*.

People assembled together to listen often weep, become emotional, and are generally moved—joy is contagious, and higher feelings spread from each person to those around them. In one hospital in South America, the patients insisted that it had been one of the most unforgettable experiences of their lives. While they listened to the mellifluous music, some moved to the beat; others held each other's hands. Something important was happening inside all of them.

9. Help if you can

If you have the opportunity, don't miss out on doing something for others. This doesn't mean collecting favors and keeping track of who's given you what or which services you've handed out to others. Few things create a greater sense of satisfaction than finding it in our power to help others. Give without asking for anything in exchange—without, of course, becoming a do-gooder. It can also be a bridge to other people. Life has many reversals and may end up surprising you.

10. **Don't be afraid of feeling vulnerable in front of someone, or of asking for help**

We don't always need to try to create strong ties in relationships; sometimes we just want a friendly hand to help us get out of a predicament. Be humble in those moments. Don't be afraid of being seen as weak or caught in a delicate situation; look for the right people, who don't judge and can give you a boost.

ASKING FOR MONEY

A few months ago, a patient told me that he had just separated from his wife. He has three children. The couple's situation was unsustainable—they were fighting every day and finally they chose to live separately. His current mental state is low, he feels somewhat depressed, and he lacks energy. At work they are restructuring, and they've lowered his salary. He doesn't have enough to give to his wife for the children, their school fees, and food.

He's moved twice and now, so as not to worry his ex-wife by failing to give her money, he is living in shared accommodation with some students. This is making him sink even further, because on the days he has his children, he avoids going home with them, not wanting them to see where he's living. He feels like a bad father; he has no money even to take them out for a treat somewhere nice. His gifts to his children are very simple, sometimes things he gets second-hand from the internet.

His father comes to my practice one day to talk to me; he's worried, because he sees that his son is sad. While he's speaking, I realize that he isn't aware, or hasn't been informed of his son's financial situation. At one point he tells me:

"He's my only child, and anything I could do for him would make me happy. My wife and I have some money saved that we don't need and maybe it would be useful to him."

Days later, I see my patient again. I tell him about my conversation with his father and he responds, "It's hard for me to ask for favors; it's hard for me to ask for money."

I explain that, in the face of the dramatic and difficult situation he finds himself in, there is no one better than his father to help him. I add that there are moments when we need to know how to lean on our support systems, without taking advantage. It was part of his therapy to be able to ask for help, but it turned out to be a determining factor in his state of mind and his relationship with his children.

11. Speak well of others; don't criticize

I'll say it again: Speak well of what is good, and maintain a neutral position about the bad. One must seriously commit to avoiding criticisms or negative judgments in conversation.

It's so nice when, during a dinner or a gathering of friends, someone holds back a criticism or halts a negative conversation about others. Speaking ill of others creates a toxic emotional state in our bodies—full of cortisol!*—and we know the risks that that brings.

Criticism is practically an international sport, and we have grown too used to it as a part of our lives. If you want people to trust you, if you want them to value you as someone with integrity, seeking out your friendship, believing in you or in your business, be discreet. Everyone in the world, despite their wrongdoing or bad attitude, has something good inside them to be redeemed. If you don't know what it is or can't see anything good in them, just leave it. Don't make the atmosphere worse by harping on a subject that doesn't seem to have a solution. In those cases, focus more on figuring out and solving the problem than on the problem itself. It's better to learn how to manage the person in question—at times it might be most convenient to distance yourself from them—than to pick them apart with your words. Not speaking ill of anyone, even

---

* In the next chapter, we'll talk about this hormone.

when people make it easy for us, produces an enormous sense of peace—it's like a sedative built into our behavioral design.

12. Tell stories

People like stories. Sometimes bringing a bit of imagination, excitement, and magic to our way of expressing ourselves can create a good ambience. For example, we know that stories are emotionally satisfying for audiences, at business meetings, and even during official councils.

Humans have always sought stories—we still seek them now and will continue to seek them in the future. Think of magicians: their way of creating rapport with the public is rooted in storytelling, and without stories their tricks have a watered-down feel to them. A great friend of mine, a magician, always wins us over with the magic, but also with his patter about the alchemical display.

Scientifically, we know that stories cause the brain to release oxytocin, a chemical substance associated with empathy and sociability. Empathy brings into play our mirror neurons. These deal with understanding the conduct and emotions of others. Discovered by Giacomo Rizzolatti, they represent a significant advance in the world of neuroscience.

A CEMENT WALL

A few years ago, two patients found themselves sharing a room in the palliative care unit of a hospital. Luis, in the bed next to the window, would talk to Daniel. Every day he would tell him, in luxuriant detail, what happened in the street. Mostly he narrated the adventures—seen from the window—of a family who lived near the hospital. The mother would often play with her children in the garden.

He spoke naturally and with grace, although his voice was slurred from the chemotherapy. For Daniel, the last months of his life were rendered entertaining by his roommate. On those days when they were alone, without family or friends, Luis would say, "Shall I tell you what I see?"

Daniel's eyes would light up. And a recital would begin that might last hours. Months later, Luis passed away, and within a few days his bed was occupied by another patient.

Daniel, excited by the thought that he would once again be able to hear the stories his friend had told him, asked his new companion to inform him about the children in their garden. The response stunned him:

"There's no garden here, just a cement wall."

Luis had used his imagination—his one remaining resource—to make up stories that would entertain Daniel.

Using empathy, Luis had been capable of putting himself in his comrade's shoes and successfully got him excited about something, helping him to overcome the suffering caused by his illness.

13.   In love and war (and friendship!), strategy is what counts

Napoleon said it. Don't be afraid to grab a pencil and a piece of paper. A four-colored ballpoint, a felt-tip pen, a blackboard . . . Write, cross out, draw arrows. Whatever you do, make a plan. You'll be surprised at how many mutual acquaintances you find, you'll discover past experiences that might be useful now, and, if you need to work on some skill because you notice it doesn't come easy, read, inform yourself, and ask for help.

There are multiple methods for improving your assertiveness and social skills. There are books and tutorials available on all of these topics. With practice, humor, and willingness, you can improve if you just decide to.

14.   Mind your manners

There are a few words that go straight to people's hearts: thank you, sorry, and please. We've gotten used to taking everything for granted. In this book, I'm going to insist on the importance that words have in our minds. Our body is not indifferent to the words we use, both in our internal monologues and in the language we employ with those around us.

15. Don't forget that in order to receive you must first give

Don't expect everything to happen without you doing your bit. Instant results are often deceptive, and you need to accept that it's difficult to build stable and durable relationships—in any area of life—in a matter of minutes. It requires patience, perseverance, and knowing how to give of yourself.

If you manage to be valued and counted on by everyone, and be someone important in their lives, you'll be pleasantly surprised to find that you're sought after, and your presence is needed in both good times and bad. People will have you on their mental radar. This goes for relationships with friends, as well as family members or business acquaintances. Try to make sure people are left with something after they see you, whether from your conversation, your way of being, or your abilities. Whatever your goal, always try to get better, to give value and to help bring the best out of others. Try to be a human vitamin, someone who adds, who helps, who brings joy and optimism even to periods of uncertainty.

Aim for a good end result, whatever your goal; when your objectives have a positive value, you attract positivity. If your ways of going deeper with people have a toxic taint, you'll attract negativity.

Don't forget, misery loves company and embittered people are surrounded by bitterness. The European Psychiatric Association describes such people as neurotic, sour, resentful, hurt, and spoiled. I've said it already in previous pages: Optimism is a powerful tool and a unique way of observing reality. Knowing how to look is also knowing how to love and understand.

16. Try to be friendly and amiable—it's more important than you think

I buy fruit at a shop right by my house. It's not especially cheap, but the grocer, Javi, helps everyone attentively. He knows our names, he treats us with a special cordiality, and every time I go, he gives a free slice of fruit to one of my children. He was away for a few months, and we all noticed his absence. When he come back, he acknowledged that he had been laid low by a serious back problem and told me what medication he was taking. It's strong medication that doesn't get rid of the pain, but does allow him to work. Impressively, he continues, despite this chronic pain, to treat everyone with the same pampering attention; he advises us on our choice of fruit and vegetables as though it were the most important choice of our lives.

People like Javi make coexisting easier and more agreeable. In a society ruled by haste, digital interaction, and time poverty, many people believe that friendliness is obsolete. We can't be bothered to stop and make an effort to greet someone or take the time to ask about their lives. The Oxford English Dictionary definition of someone who is amiable describes them as "friendly, lovable, likable." You almost gasp reading it—it's too perfect!

There are people whose amiability seems to be hardwired into their genes. They almost don't need to try—it flows out of them so naturally. Being amiable means being capable of communicating cordiality and sympathy, of treating others with dignity. Let us not forget that people possess a "friendliness gene" from their earliest days. This tool influences us in an important way. For example, when faced with stress, adversity, or dangerous situations, having worked on this ability leads us to care for and help others, instead of only looking after our own survival or well-being. Another fact: Among people who have suffered a stroke, those who perceive affection and amiability around them feel less pain than those who find themselves alone.

We know of more benefits from friendliness, besides just those that improve our relationships. This touches once more on a biochemical element that we will discuss in depth in this book. Amiability generates endorphins, which in turn lower levels of cortisol—the stress and anxiety hormone—and increase oxytocin—the love and trust hormone. As a consequence, hypertension and cardiovascular problems are ameliorated and painful sensations diminish. All these effects create in us a feeling of balance and internal well-being. Simply observing friendly people—even in films—improves our mood and has significant physiological effects.

Of course, to everything there is a season! If someone struggles to be friendly, affectionate, or intimate, they should practice little by little. You should avoid seeming phony; very few things provoke more repulsion than a sense that someone is faking or being hypocritical. Nor should one confuse friendliness with naïveté or being a do-gooder or a martyr. Faced with an attack, a rejection, or an aggression, one must know how to detach, take some space, and note any damage sustained.

CASE STUDY: SUSANA

Susana studied as an optician and works in her cousin's pharmacy in Valencia. She's married to Jorge, a hard-working man who owns car dealerships with his siblings. They have two children, one and five years old.

When Susana comes to my office, she tells me that her husband has left. She's devastated "because my marriage was working very well, we hardly argued at all, and I don't understand what could have happened." According to what she tells me, nothing out of the ordinary occurred; Jorge simply told her one day that he couldn't take it anymore and left. She insists the relationship between them was good and that their marriage was envied by many. When asked if there was someone else, she responds that she's sure there must be, but that he denies it. We start to unpack Susana's character and life story, and we uncover a woman with a big heart—lovable, warm, a friend to everyone. She's always caring for those around her.

Her father is a man of strong character; he's impulsive, but she knows how to get along with him and, when everything looks like it's going to fall apart, she knows how to salvage the situation. When she tells me about the last few years of her marriage to Jorge, I detect a certain lack of respect on his part: he humiliated her, made absurd demands, and had various manias. On the weekend, he wanted the house to be clean and would yell at Susana to wash the glasses or the floor over and over. She, with her habitual desire to accommodate, would obey in order to make him happy, without realizing that the relationship had become a dictatorship, where she had undertaken to make his life agreeable without reflecting. Susana described it to me like this: "I've always been friendly, intimate, and affectionate with my loved ones, without thinking too much—that's the key to good relationships."

Evidently, Susana is right, but if you don't know how to measure the degree of amiability that you show, you can end up becoming the victim of someone who uses or manipulates you. There are people who will take advantage of this personality type in the most scandalous way!

What the World Needs Now Is . . . Oxytocin

This hormone plays a fundamental role in birth, labor, and lactation. It's the hormone that triggers the body to push out the baby when undergoing labor, as well as acting as a signal to let down milk during the postpartum period. We know that this hormone is foundational in two primordial phenomena of emotional life: trust and empathy. For this reason, it's an essential tool in social relations, and in our way of interacting with others.

Both being friendly and presenting yourself in a positive way can activate oxytocin, which has marvelous effects on our body: It diminishes sensations of anxiety, it protects the heart, and it even lowers cholesterol levels.

Company Agrees with Us: Oxytocin and Dopamine

Two hormones are secreted when we're in good company and enjoying life along with people we love: oxytocin, mentioned above, and dopamine—the pleasure hormone. Research is currently underway into the applications of oxytocin sprays or vaporizers for people with autism, but the results of the first experiments are as yet inconclusive.

Oxytocin may also be a key factor in the world of business and economics. In an article published in the journals *Nature* and *Neuron*, the director of the Institute for Empirical Research in Economics at the University of Zurich, Ernst Fehr, demonstrated that oxytocin boosted people's ability to trust their money, inheritance, or savings to others. They observed that participants in the experiment who had been stimulated with oxytocin trusted their money to others more easily than those who had received a placebo; 45% of the first group agreed to invest a large sum of money, while of the second group only 21% did.

When a person's oxytocin levels rise above normal, emotions like love, empathy and compassion grow more intense. It has even been observed that in those cases where the hormone is really through the roof, it becomes more difficult for people to stay resentful or annoyed. When oxytocin is elevated, the amygdala—the area of the brain in charge of fear—is deactivated, and therefore anxiety, anguish, and obsessive and negative thoughts diminish in intensity.

With this in mind, have a go at being nice. During the next few weeks, choose a person you find difficult and try to create a more agreeable connection with them. Search out those people with whom you spend a lot of time, and try to make the relationship closer; smile, try not to judge so much, and—knowing what's at stake, and that if you make a good faith effort you might change your brain, your emotions, and your biochemistry—try to love more, love better, and be more compassionate toward those around you!

Your life is measured not by what you receive but by what you give. I often ask my patients, "What do you do for others?"

Pay more attention to your relationships, from your family to your friends, your colleagues, and even your neighbors. Invest in people, for real. If you do it authentically with affection, it won't wear you out as much as you think. Show up and offer your help sincerely, and not with a generic "whatever you need" that doesn't really mean anything. In a society where loneliness and isolation are on the rise, look for ways to step out of yourself.

LOVE OF IDEALS AND BELIEFS

We have ideas, but we are situated in our beliefs.

—José Ortega y Gasset

We all know of people who have survived terrible trials, sustained by their love for their ideals. From Nelson Mandela on Robben Island—love for his people—to Thomas More in the Tower of London—his beliefs—or even Maximilian Kolbe, giving his life for another man's—the father of a family—in the concentration camp at Auschwitz. Or think of Russian soldiers in World War II, who endured adverse conditions and battlefields where the temperature was 20 degrees below zero, for love of their country. Everyone has their own ideals, and if they're strong, they can become allies in times of suffering.

Viktor Frankl is a great teacher in many ways. He suffered in Nazi concentration camps and analyzed the "psychopathology of the masses" in World War II. He emphasizes one idea above all: you can take absolutely everything away from a man, except the last of his human freedoms, which is the choice of his attitude toward life. This is where memories, values, and ideals come into play. With the right attitude, one can choose one's own destiny, despite circumstances. This inner freedom, which cannot be taken from us, allows us to find meaning in our lives, whatever our circumstances. Even in the concentration camps during World War II, there were people who, holding fast to that inner freedom, knew how to rise above the atrocities that surrounded them.

Viktor Frankl didn't know about the biochemical aspects of passion and hope, but he observed that when somebody had memories or ideals to cling to, that person was capable of surviving any type of trauma, both physically and psychologically. Having ideals, and keeping hold of pleasant memories to return to when oppressed by circumstance, can constitute a significant support for confronting problems that arise in the future.

Of course, be careful with extremist ideals! Extremism justifies any idea or action as a means to a certain end. Extremist reasoning confers legitimacy on anything, including true barbarities lacking any moral value, as long as it helps reach an ultimate goal. It is right that our system of values should serve as our compass for navigating life, a guide for our behavior. But extremism has become a problem if, on the path to our legitimate goal, we ride roughshod over others. A person with radical ideas is not only incapable of understanding and respecting other people's convictions but eventually justifies any infringement on others' rights if it brings them closer to their desired end.

As Einstein aptly said, "Worry more about your conscience than your reputation. Your conscience is what you are, your reputation is only what others think of you."

LOVE OF MEMORIES

There are moments in life whose memory is enough to erase years of suffering.

—Voltaire

Are you surprised to learn that a cherished memory can mitigate suffering?

To continue with Viktor Frankl, he observed that there were people in Auschwitz who died a few days after arriving, regardless of their physical state, and others who endured for long periods, though they seemed no stronger than those who had succumbed first. His own experience in the extermination camp confirmed his new theory of logotherapy, which he had been studying since before the war. Those people whose lives had meaning were better able to tolerate the suffering of Auschwitz.

How can we interpret this, adapting it to the conditions of modern life?

*People who find an aim, a goal, and a meaning
in their lives have more reasons to be happy.*

There are so many people who can't find a reason to get up in the morning!

If your thoughts and memories are constantly connected back to the people you love, special moments, or things you're looking forward to, you'll be happier and more joyful. Careful—this doesn't always come naturally, and sometimes you have to fight for it! We must be capable of reflection, of thinking about our lives and finding in them those people, moments, or hopes that we can turn into our motivations. There are a lot of people who let themselves go, who don't search within themselves, who simply let themselves be carried along day after day.

We're touching on an important subject here. Remembering agreeable scenes has a strong impact on the brain: the act of recalling special moments from the past can produce the same substances and activate the same areas of the brain that were activated when these things happened in reality. This constitutes, in my opinion, the beginning of a genuine revolution in the world of neuroscience.

Dr. Herbert Benson, a physician, cardiologist, and professor at Harvard, was one of the first Western scientists to thoroughly explore relaxation and meditation, inspired by Eastern philosophy. He is a pioneer in the study of mind and body, or what he calls "behavioral medicine." His objective is to demonstrate the value of meditation and certain mental attitudes in facing the pernicious effects of anxiety and stress. His ideas form a bridge between religion and medicine, faith and science, uniting East and West, mind and body. Dr. Benson has a name for this concept: remembered wellness. Recalling gratifying, moving, or joyful past events allows our bodies to release biochemical substances with antidepressant effects.

When I perceive tension within a couple, I usually ask, "How did you meet? How did you fall in love with your husband?"

Even with a build-up of annoyance and tension, the act of remembering joyful past events manages to change, at least for a brief time, the emotional tone of the person speaking. For this reason, many relaxation techniques or cures for stress or trauma create what we call a "safe space" in the mind. This is a sensation, memory, or image that gives us a feeling of peace, simply by calling it to mind.

Dr. Benson maintains that a person with a headache or back pain can get better just with a placebo. The cause? Remembering the sensation of well-being they felt after ingesting medication. This is why the placebo effect is so magically potent, as we all know.

SUSUMU TONEGAWA:
THE SCIENTIFIC POWER OF A HAPPY MEMORY

The Japanese molecular biologist, Susumu Tonegawa, was awarded the Nobel Prize in Medicine in 1987 for discovering the genetic mechanism that produces the body's entire range of antibodies—this constituted a huge advance in immune research. In 1990, he abruptly changed his field of study and began deepening his knowledge of the molecular basis for memory formation and recall. Two years later, he discovered an enzyme that he named CaMKII—calmodulin-dependent protein kinase II—involved in the transduction of signals between cells and an essential mediator in learning and memory processes. Poor regulation of this enzyme is associated with Alzheimer's.

An investigation led by Tonegawa at MIT, published in the journal *Nature* in 2017, postulated that recalling past events has a beneficial effect on an individual's state of mind because it activates both their reward and motivation systems.

Bringing positive experiences from the past to mind serves as a powerful antidote to depression and other disordered mental states. That might not come as much of a surprise, but it's comforting to know that this common-sense advice has a verified neuroscientific basis.

Various areas of the brain are involved in this process: on the one hand, the hippocampus (the memory zone par excellence); the amygdala (which manages fear and recalls experiences with elevated emotional content); and the nucleus accumbens (our reward system).

Memories have a healing power even greater than that of positive experiences themselves.

3

CORTISOL

Thinking alters our internal world. Imagine that you're in a cinema or a theater and you hear someone shout, "Fire!"

You'd immediately be on the alert and start running for the nearest exit in a panic.

What's happening in your body in that moment? The startled body sends a signal to the hypothalamus, which, in turn, activates other areas of the brain. An involuntary response is triggered through hormonal and nerve signals—the mind may not even have become aware of the danger yet—giving rise to tachycardia, sweating, and an increase in temperature, as we have all experienced at one time or another. This information passes through the thalamus and the cerebral cortex, where it's processed cognitively, and the brain makes a decision, as rationally as the feeling of fear will allow it, about how to respond to the threat.

Next, the suprarenal glands, located above the kidneys, having received the signal from the hypothalamus, release a series of hormones—among these, we want to pay particular attention to adrenaline and cortisol.

GET TO KNOW YOUR TRAVELING COMPANION

I'm now going to introduce you to one of life's most important traveling companions. Once you've read the next few pages, you'll understand why certain things happen to you, you're going to understand certain experiences you've had, and you're going to comprehend much of the behavior of those around you. Pay special attention to this chapter.

> *Cortisol isn't harmful in itself—what's*
> *bad for us is an excess of cortisol.*

Let's continue our story. We're still in the cinema. If cortisol wasn't involved, we'd probably stay in our seats enjoying the spectacle of smoke and flames. Cortisol is therefore fundamental to survival.

Imagine, on the other hand, the real situation. You get up from your seat, experiencing tachycardia, hyperventilation, and a feeling of distress, and you look for the nearest exit. You see the frightened faces of those around you; you're finding it difficult to think clearly. Finally, you succeed in getting out to the street, sweating and trembling. Once you're outside, someone tells you that there's no need to worry, they're adjusting the alarm system and it went off for no reason—there's no fire. In that moment, the doors are opened again and ten minutes later the whole audience has taken their places again. In one sense, everyone has returned to their original positions, but in reality nobody is in the same physiological or mental condition as before the alarm went off.

Why? That shot of cortisol that we received will take several hours to disappear completely and return to its normal levels. It must have happened to you at some point, perhaps while driving: Someone passes you with a clumsy maneuver, and although nothing happens and you don't collide, your body nonetheless perceives a threat and your heart starts racing. But nothing happened! This is your body's warning signal.

What, then, is cortisol's function?

- Cortisol has a profound effect on multiple systems within the body. When our cortisol levels are elevated, we are ready to start running; our blood travels from our intestines to our muscles to help strengthen our evasive or defensive actions, which is why we lose our appetites at moments of distress. The senses are activated ("My nerves are on a knife's edge"), trying to detect any stimulus that would help us to identify an intuited threat. Our musculature receives the necessary signals (nerve signals as well as biochemical ones) to prepare for either evading the danger or fighting the danger. Cortisol helps oxygen, glucose and fatty acids to fulfill their respective functions in the muscles. An elevated heart rate means the heart beats faster, facilitating the circulation of the blood and the nutrients it carries to the muscles, so that these can respond in the face of the eventual threat.
- Cortisol also inhibits the secretion of insulin, provoking the release of glucose and proteins into the blood. Because of this, if cortisol isn't properly regulated, it doesn't take long before the dreaded diabetes can appear.
- This hormone helps to regulate the body's osmotic system, its fluids. This is key for controlling blood pressure and has an impact on the bones (cortisol can heighten the chances of developing osteoporosis) and muscles as well (spasms, stitches, cramps, and so on).
- Cortisol has an essential function: It profoundly affects the immune system, inhibiting inflammation (to begin with). We'll look at this in more detail, because it's indispensable for understanding the appearance of certain serious illnesses. When dealing with stress, the body saves its energy resources. The immune system requires a huge quantity of energy; that's why you feel worn out when you're ill—most of your energy is being channelled into your defense system.
- Finally, cortisol alters various systems on an endocrinological level:
  - The reproductive system: stress and suffering can change a woman's normal cycle or affect her ability to get pregnant.

- o   The body's growth system can be inhibited.
- o   The thyroid system can become irregular (hyper or hypothyroidism), or other illnesses related to this gland can arise.

To all of this can be added a factor that relates to the body's growth. Faced with an imminent threat, your body requires all of its stored energy. To capture it, it paralyzes and blocks anything judged dispensable, including the functions that have to do with growth. Millions of cells die every day, and human beings require daily cellular regeneration, but if we interfere—due to stress—with the growth of these cells, the body will fall ill, having failed to replace the cells it loses.

WHAT HAPPENS IF YOU RETURN TO THE SITE OF A TRAUMATIC EVENT?

Some time later you return to the same theater. You sit down in the same seat and suddenly, you don't know why, you're on high alert. You get up and do a visual scan for the emergency exit. Then you have second thoughts about the seat you've chosen and change places so that you're closer to the door. What's happening is that you're reliving the distress of the previous occasion. At that moment, your body is generating the same amount of cortisol that was produced when the alarm really went off.

Your mind and body can't distinguish reality from imagination.

The brain, therefore, has a profound effect on our inner equilibrium. When we think of things that worry us, those thoughts have a similar impact to the real situations. Every time we imagine something we find overwhelming, our organism's warning system is activated, and cortisol is released, because our body thinks it's necessary to face up to the threat.

WHAT HAPPENS IF YOU LIVE
WITH CONSTANT ANXIETY?

Prolonged worries or feelings of danger—whether real or imagined—can push cortisol levels up to 50 percent higher than what they should be. This fact is fundamental to understanding stress: real dangers and threats aren't the only ones that trigger the body. It's also activated, and in exactly the same way, by anxiety about losing a job, a friendship, or a possession; or by the possibility that our status, our position in the community, or our role in a group is in question.

Cortisol is a cyclical hormone: during the night, levels decrease, then ascend to a peak at about eight in the morning, then steadily decrease again. The release of cortisol follows a pattern, which is usually tied to the rhythm of daylight: more is released on waking, which has a beneficial effect on our ability to be active in the morning; then it decreases over the course of the day and rises again slightly as night falls.

*When cortisol levels are chronically
elevated, it begins to act as a toxin.*

Stress is one of the dominant factors that dictates the body's inflammatory response. Through the three main circuits of the body—endocrine, immune, and neuronal—stress provokes substantial modifications in the correct functioning of the systems involved in the inflammatory process.

- In the endocrine system, the body responds by activating the release of cortisol and norepinephrine. If someone gets "toxified" by the levels of cortisol in their blood, an alteration occurs in their inflammatory response.
- The immune system also has an important relationship to inflammatory response. The defense cells, which have specific cortisol receptors in their membrane, become more sensitive and stop being able to control inflammation as precisely.

- The nervous system is responsible for preparing and coordinating the body's response to a threat or a danger. The brain, by means of the peripheral nervous system (the sympathetic nervous system holds an important function), aided by the hormonal system (cortisol), puts the rest of the body on alert. These signals will allow for the changes in our organism referred to above, in order to adapt to the danger. If stress becomes chronic, the adaptation and reaction mechanisms become saturated, and a neurological block can arise, resulting in various illnesses.

A person under constant stress struggles with two main problems: on the one hand, the healthy growth and regeneration functions of the body are halted, and on the other hand, the immune system is inhibited.

UNDERSTANDING THE NERVOUS SYSTEM

The vegetative nervous system is formed by the ensemble of neurons that regulate our involuntary functions. This system is in turn subdivided into the sympathetic and parasympathetic nervous systems, two completely antagonistic systems—the first is involved in action, and the second in repose.

The Sympathetic Nervous System

This system has to do with our survival instincts, and the behaviors that are activated at moments of high alert. It triggers mechanisms for accelerating and strengthening cardiac rhythm, and stimulates capillary erection and perspiration. It facilitates voluntary muscular contraction, provokes bronchial dilation in order to promote rapid oxygenation, and encourages the constriction of the blood vessels, redirecting blood away from the internal organs toward the muscles and the heart. It provokes the dilation of our pupils, so we can scan our surroundings more easily, and triggers the release of adrenaline and cortisol from the adrenal glands. All of this is very handy for staying alert in unfamiliar situations, where we feel uncertain or our personal safety is under threat. If it becomes necessary to flee, it's convenient for the blood not to be tied up in our digestive system, but available to the muscles in our extremities—we'll have time enough to digest when we've reached a place of safety, away from the threat bearing down on us.

The sympathetic system is, therefore, key to the stress reaction that occurs when faced with the unknown, the unfamiliar, or something out of our control. But the constant activation of this system can have very harmful effects on our health because it impedes the regeneration of tissues that aid the function of the parasympathetic system, among other reasons.

The Parasympathetic Nervous System

This prioritizes activating the peristaltic functions and secretions of the digestive and urinary apparatuses. It enables the relaxation of sphincters, allowing for the evacuation of excrement and urine, and provokes bronchial constriction and respiratory secretion. It foments vascular dilation, in order to redistribute the flow of blood toward the internal organs; it encourages sexual excitement; and is responsible for a diminution in the force and frequency of the heart's muscular contractions. In general, the parasympathetic nervous system is involved in the maintenance of cells and tissues, preventing or reducing their deterioration, so that we can live longer and in better condition.

SYMPTOMS CAUSED BY "TOXIC CORTISOL"

Life as it is currently lived is more "inflammatory" than ever before.

Chronic stress reduces the sensitivity of immune cells to cortisol. That is to say, the body's defense system is deactivated and incapable of combating a real threat. The capacity to regulate inflammation has been reined in, and therefore the body is incapable of defending us from danger. In fact, threatening situations or situations that provoke tension or fear can activate substances—prostaglandins, leukotrienes, cytokines—that can be very damaging to our tissues. This is the reason that we're more prone to contract infections at certain times. Who hasn't experienced an illness coming on a few days after the start of a holiday? Our body grows weak and gives way to a cold, a urinary tract infection, or gastroenteritis.

This cortisol-immune system alteration occurs even on a genetic level. We know that "toxic cortisol" can modify us even at the deepest levels. "New" cells, arriving from the bone marrow, will be insensitive to cortisol from their birth. This can become the cause of many illnesses and disorders that are currently widespread. In today's world, we're effectively living through an experiment.

The mere idea of being threatened increases the production of inflammatory cytokines, proteins that can be very damaging to certain cells in the body. This is usually associated with a reduction in the cells of the immune system, which makes us more liable to contract infections.

The opposite is also true! When, instead of feeling threatened by others, we feel understood, and we cooperate with those around us, the vagus nerve, which forms part of the parasympathetic system, is activated.

What happens when cortisol levels remain elevated for a prolonged period because of stress or any kind of problem, fear, or tension? People who live in a constant state of stress, high alert, or apprehension suffer more cellular deterioration and premature aging. We now know that many illnesses are initiated following periods of chronic stress, during which people live constantly with such feelings.

Cortisol levels, as I've explained, rise in circumstances that provoke fear, a sense of danger, sadness, or frustration. If we're "toxified" by cortisol, the hormone will inundate our blood in the place of serotonin or dopamine, hormones that have a positive impact on mental and physical wellbeing.

The symptomatology of this condition manifests on three levels: physical, psychological, and behavioral.

Physical Symptoms

I'll list a few symptoms: alopecia (hair loss), uncontrollable blinking, excessive perspiration of the hands and feet, dry skin, feeling a lump in the throat, tightness in the chest, a feeling of suffocation, tachycardia (fast heart rate), paraesthesia (getting a dead arm or leg), gastrointestinal problems or alterations, irritable bowel syndrome, muscular pain, thyroid problems, migraines, tics, arthritis, fibromyalgia ...

It's very common among women to see irregularities in the menstrual cycle; as the hormones responsible are particularly sensitive to stress.

Why Does Everything Hurt?

Bumping into things, cutting yourself, falling over—these accidents are part of all our lives. The body responds to such mishaps by triggering self-healing mechanisms, one of which is inflammation. This is a good, healthy response—it prevents infections and further harm, helping to repair any damage done to cells and tissues. Muscular stiffness (which makes fiber ruptures more likely), a constant sensation of pain, heaviness, tightness, or contraction is something we've all experienced: All of these have an explanation whose final cause isn't always to be found in the locomotive apparatus. Chronic stress, a lack of healthy exercise, or poor nutrition are some of the causes of this constant pain. This is one of the reasons for the current rise in overuse of NSAIDs, or anti-inflammatory medications such as ibuprofen.

Muscular pains are not due solely to inflammation triggered by the adrenal-cortisol-immune mechanism; they are also caused by the activation of the sympathetic nervous system, which forces the body to adopt a defensive posture. Sometimes muscular discomfort is very intense around the jaw area—a disruption of the temporomandibular joint (TMJ). This pain arises due to a constant grinding movement of the teeth—bruxism—that finishes by wearing them down and damaging the joint. Bruxism is especially intense at night. It's now very common to sleep with a dental apparatus adapted to deal with the problem.

Psychological Symptoms

Changes can occur in sleep patterns—we'll devote a section to this—along with an increase in irritability, sadness, inability to enjoy things, aimlessness, and apathy. In a permanent state of alert, lapses in concentration, memory, or other mental functions occur. Permanent anxiety opens the door to depression. Many instances of depression come from living in a state of high alert for long periods of time.

Our memories are very sensitive to cortisol levels. The hippocampus is the area of the brain responsible for learning and memory, and it's directly affected by changes in cortisol levels. I'm sure this has happened to you: you arrive at an exam, more or less prepared but very nervous, and your mind goes blank. But you studied for it! This is easily explained: what's happened is that your hippocampus is blocked by a sudden rise in cortisol. Anticipatory nerves, stemming from worries like "I might fail, I don't know what's going to happen, I can't remember, they're sure to ask about the things I didn't review" block the hippocampus and the memory, meaning that our fears, unfounded to begin with, end up becoming reality.

Behavioral Symptoms

High levels of cortisol encourage us to isolate ourselves; it's no longer tempting to see friends or relatives, initiating a conversation is difficult, and we begin to avoid our habitual activities. We also might not engage at social events or feel the desire to open ourselves up to others.

> *Physiological stress—eustress—is neither harmful*
> *nor toxic. On the contrary, it's our body's natural*
> *response to a real or imagined threat, indispensable*
> *for our survival at moments of danger, which helps*
> *us to respond in the best possible way to challenges.*
> *It becomes harmful when the threat disappears or*

is revealed to be unfounded, but the mind and body
continue to experience a sensation of danger or fear.

MY MIND AND MY BODY CAN'T
TELL TRUTH FROM FICTION

This is another of the main ideas I want to get across with this book. The brain doesn't know how to differentiate what is real from what is imaginary. Every time we modify our mental state—consciously or unconsciously—a change occurs in the body that is as much molecular as cellular and genetic. In the same way, when we modify our physical state, the mind and the emotions take note. I've highlighted over and over in this chapter the importance of being conscious of one's thoughts. Thinking alters our body. The mind adapts and reconfigures according to the changing factors, circumstances, and experiences of each day.

A stressed-out brain is the consequence of
being inundated with toxic thoughts.

The mind has an extraordinary degree of control and influence over the body. Thoughts directly influence both mind and body. If you close your eyes and picture someone you love, in a nice setting, your body secretes oxytocin and dopamine. You might even feel a shiver run through your body, or get goose bumps or a number of other physical signs. People in love (I could write an entire separate book about people in love!) experience a very strong sensation of emotional, psychological, and (especially) physical wellbeing. If I imagine something that frightens me—an exam, a meeting, the possibility of getting fired or not having money—I automatically generate stress hormones.

I'll give you a basic example. Close your eyes and visualize a lemon. It's yellow, ovoid, etc. Feel it in your hand, really touch it. Bring it to your nose. Take a knife and cut it open. What do you observe? Have you started salivating yet? Cut a slice and bring it to your lips, taste it, take a risk and bite into it. Open your eyes, and of course the lemon isn't there—but your body reacted as though it were. The imagination has significant power over the mind.

Your thoughts exercise great power over your brain and your body. If you run over a past event or a negative future possibility in your mind again and again, your brain understands it as present in your current situation, getting in the way of what you want to focus on. What happens? Your attention is always hooked, and you're imprisoned by toxic thoughts of the past or the future; that is to say, the mind can't successfully manage and focus its attention as it wants to. To express this more visually, every time we think of something negative, worrying, or harmful, the brain receives a signal to develop specialized neural circuits that will keep us locked into these ideas. The mind cannot tell truth from fiction. Later we'll look at practical tips for permanently redirecting our thoughts and controlling the current of negative ideas that can block up our minds.

NUTRITION, INFLAMMATION, AND CORTISOL

Some say that we are what we eat. I'm more inclined to believe that we are what we feel, what we think, and what we love—but I'm aware that nutrition plays a fundamental role in our health. We know that some foods have a significant correlation to certain serious illnesses, such as cancer, and it's therefore something we shouldn't ignore. In recent years, our dietary habits have visibly shifted. Currently, according to data used by nutritional specialists, the average person ingests 30 percent more pro-inflammatory food than a few years ago.

People with chronic inflammation have lower than recommended levels of certain vitamins—C, D, and E—and omega-3. In addition, persistent inflammation alters the intestinal barrier, leading to a greater degree of permeability to certain substances. This finishes by harming the immune system and can lead to discomfort and adverse reactions after ingesting certain foods.

Foods that activate inflammation have a strong correlation to the release of insulin by the pancreas; among the "usual suspects" are alcohol—especially in large doses—saturated fats, sugary drinks, and refined flours, above all those used in industrial baking.

Be careful with inflammatory fast food. According to a recently published Harvard study, women with a diet rich in inflammatory ingredients—white flour, saturated and trans fats, sugary drinks, and red meat—have a 41 percent greater chance of suffering from depression. We must reintroduce those foods that have an anti-inflammatory effect into our diets, such as:

- Omega-3 (which we'll discuss in more detail in Chapter 8)
- Some spices such as turmeric, which has powerful anti-inflammatory properties
- Citrus
- Vitamin D. More and more studies connect depression to low vitamin D levels. We psychiatrists are beginning to evaluate vitamin D levels in our patients, and we've observed an improvement in depressive symptoms after treatment with vitamin D.
- Onions, leeks, parsley, bay leaves, and rosemary. In fact, in some cases of injury to the foot or ankle, soaking the foot in water infused with bay leaf and rosemary has a beneficial effect on diminishing inflammation.

WHAT ROLE DOES THE DIGESTIVE SYSTEM PLAY IN INFLAMMATION?

A couple of years ago I was asked to be involved in a study on probiotics and intestinal flora and their direct relationship to emotional and mental states. I got hold of a lot of information on the topic, reading articles and publications on the theme. It's an exciting field, with many discoveries still ahead, and in the last few years studies in this area have multiplied.

A significant connection prevails between the brain and the intestines.

The digestive tract, comprising the whole stretch from the esophagus to the anus, is carpeted in over a hundred million nerve cells—that's an equivalent amount to the entirety of the brain's central nervous system, from the cerebellum to the spine! In addition, more than a hundred billion microorganisms are contained inside the digestive tract. They fulfill an important function in the processing of food and nutrients, releasing a huge quantity of molecules into the intestines. These can eventually influence the body in a fundamental way.

Investigation in this area is recent, and in research terms, the field is still a baby in diapers, but the first studies published on the topic, based on experiments with mice, show that a lack of bacterial flora has important repercussions on the body, including the brain. Special attention is being paid to the relationship of cause and effect between certain sudden changes to bacterial flora and simultaneous alterations in a patient's conduct or state of mind.

There are many theories. A review published in 2015 (Kelly et al.) suggests that deficits in the permeability of the intestine might be the cause of the inflammation that appears in conjunction with emotional disturbances. Elsewhere, it's been postulated that some microorganisms secrete substances that perform the same tasks as neurotransmitters in the brain. Finally, there are speculations that some of the substances produced by these microorganisms in the digestive tract directly affect the immune system or the nervous system.

Microbiota have a fundamental role in the regulation of intestinal permeability and in the inflammatory aspect of depression.

Serotonin, the happiness and well-being hormone implicated in appetite, libido, and many other mental and physical functions, is responsible for a state of anxiety or depression. But it would be a mistake to reduce depression simply to *cerebral* serotonin levels. Approximately 90 percent of the body's serotonin is produced in the intestines, and the rest in the brain.

More research into probiotics and mental states is constantly emerging. In December 2017, a study was published in the journal *Brain, Behavior, and Immunity* about how probiotics counteract depressive tendencies. At the University of Aarhus, researchers highlighted the benefits of probiotics not only to intestinal health but to subjects' state of mind.

Recently a study led by Dr. Nicola Lopizzo was published, which drew a connection between Alzheimer's disease and inflammation and microbiota. She observed that the sick individuals had different microbiota from the healthy subjects who participated in the study. It's now being postulated that inflammation plays a key role in the development and evolution of Alzheimer's. It is believed that inflammation can be influenced by a body's microbiota. This is an exciting field, and there's a push to further research in this direction.

IS DEPRESSION AN INFLAMMATORY ILLNESS OF THE BRAIN?

Based on everything we've read and understood up to this point, we know that there's an important relationship between inflammation, especially chronic inflammation, and illness. But what happens with depression? What role does inflammation play in depressive processes?

In recent years, various voices have been heard within the scientific community attempting to explain this relationship, something I find very exciting. In the February 2018 edition of the prestigious journal *Lancet*, Dr. Jeff Meyer's team published the first scientific evidence of inflammation's role in depression. After an exhaustive image analysis—using positron emission tomography, or PET scans—it was observed that people who had suffered from depression for years showed alterations to their brains, with an increase in inflammatory cells, which is to say an excessive immune response.

In addition, it has been observed that after administering certain immunomodulatory pharmaceuticals, such as interferon alpha (IFN-α), for the treatment of multiple sclerosis, melanoma, hepatitis C, and other illnesses, many subjects presented comorbidity in the form of depressive symptoms.

What happens when children suffer violence, trauma, serious wounds, and bullying?

Recent studies (Cattaneo, 2015), suggest that childhood stress—bullying, separation from parents, physical or psychological abuse—provokes inflammatory processes that can make children more likely to suffer from emotional disturbances and greater vulnerability, and can even provoke depression in adulthood. This can now be "measured" in the blood. We mustn't forget that one of the main problems in the diagnosis and treatment of depression is a lack of markers that allow us to confront it in a personalized, specific way. One of the most trustworthy parameters in this regard is the presence of C-reactive protein in the blood.

Elevated levels of C-reactive protein (CRP) in the blood are connected to a lack of energy and alterations in sleep patterns and appetite.

It's reasonable to offer alternatives to patients who don't respond to known antidepressants. One solution may reside in the measuring levels of inflammatory markers like IL-6, TNF-alpha and CRP. We know that these can be trustworthy markers in the diagnosis and monitoring of depression; people suffering from depression have almost 50 percent more C-reactive protein than others.

Chronic, sustained, low-grade inflammation is a key player when it comes to the likelihood of developing depression or psychosis.

In October 2016, an article was published in the journal *Molecular Psychiatry*, by Dr. Golam Khandaker of the Cambridge University Psychiatry Department. The article studied the effects of applying anti-inflammatories to depression. Researchers employed anti-cytokine pharmaceuticals—anti-inflammatory molecules—to treat autoimmune inflammatory illnesses. When they collected their results and analyzed the secondary effects, they noticed with surprise that there was an improvement in depressive symptoms.

Pharmacological treatments are far from infallible: a third of patients don't respond to the antidepressants currently on the market. Faced with this treatment gap, inflammation seems to be an essential factor for many people suffering from depression. Perhaps in the not-too-distant future, it will be possible to prescribe anti-inflammatory pharmaceuticals* to patients resistant to conventional treatments for depression. We would be talking about biological anti-inflammatories, similar to those used on auto-immune diseases—anti-cytokine monoclonal antibodies.

Around a third of patients who do not respond to conventional antidepressants show clear evidence of inflammation.

To sum up:

- Depression goes hand in hand with chronic low-grade inflammation linked to immune system activation (caused by cytokines and other substances).
- Depression frequently presents along with inflammatory illnesses, cardiovascular ailments, and cancer.
- The application of some immunomodulatory pharmaceuticals produces depressive symptoms.
- Diabetes sufferers are twice as likely to suffer from depression.
- We now know that stress, tobacco, digestive modifications, and low vitamin D levels are accompanied by an inflammatory response.

---

* This doesn't mean commonly used anti-inflammatory medications such as ibuprofen, but they are similar, although they deal specifically with the biochemical aspects of the inflammatory processes of depression.

Inflammation doesn't just trigger the beginnings of depression—it's also a key factor in its remission.

- Inflammation is a key process of depression. It needs to be taken into account at several different points: as a marker of the illness but also as a response to treatment. It can be useful to monitor the levels of inflammation over the course of treatment, to take note of its possible resistance or response.

- Studying inflammation has opened up a new world of possibilities in the care of depression resistant to conventional treatments.

- Inflammation is key to understanding and finding the links between coexisting symptoms and organic disorders (such as cardiovascular illnesses and depression, chronic anxiety, and endocrine disorders.).

- When we get ill, we generate substances that alert the body that something isn't working: cytokines. With depression, cytokine levels increase notably. With other mental illnesses, such as bipolar disorder, we know that cytokine levels stabilize during periods of remission.

4

NEITHER WHAT HAS BEEN
NOR WHAT IS TO COME

HEALING THE WOUNDS OF THE PAST AND GETTING EXCITED FOR THE FUTURE

As a psychiatrist, I usually define happiness as the capacity to live healthily, anchored in the present, having overcome the wounds of the past and looking hopefully toward the future. People who spend their lives stuck in the past are depressive, neurotic, and embittered; people who spend their lives terrified for the future are anxious. Depression and anxiety are the major illnesses of the twenty-first century.

> *At least 90 percent of what we worry about never happens, but the body and the mind live through these anxieties as though they were real.*

We live in a constant state of bombardment, worried by things that aren't particularly likely to happen. What if I don't pass this test? What if I get made redundant? What if I don't get a place at university? What if I don't finish this project? What if they don't renew my scholarship? What if my partner leaves me? What if something happens to my children? What if I get sick? What if my parents get sick? This recurrent "what if" has a strong effect on the body and mind. Don't forget that you can only act, feel, and respond in the present moment. You must take responsibility for your actions in each moment, for your capacity to proceed in the here and now.

If you ask someone what's worrying them, their
response will be about the past or the future—
we've forgotten how to live in the present!

Living Stuck in the Past

The past is a valuable source of information, but it doesn't determine your future. The act of living with your mind anchored in the past, turning over and over things that have already happened, can have adverse effects, bringing up emotions and sensations from melancholy, frustration, guilt, sadness, or resentment all the way to full-blown depression.

All of these have an element in common—they prevent us from enjoying the present. Getting stuck in the past prevents us from moving forward in life.

GUILT

Few emotions can be as toxic and destructive as guilt. Guilt consists in the feeling that we haven't acted correctly or haven't fulfilled what was expected of us, thereby disappointing other people—or ourselves.

Guilt can have a range of origins or causes: the level of demands placed on us by others or by ourselves, what we're taught by our parents, taboos, school, our relationships to our classmates or colleagues, sexual feelings that have been malformed or misdirected in childhood and adolescence, or incorrect or extreme interpretations of religious teachings. Guilt, therefore, has various focal points:

- It can come from inside you. In this case you are always turning your mind towards failures and disappointments. Your gaze is directed inward to your limitations and mistakes. You treat yourself with disdain, with a harshness that prevents you from moving forward and seeing the positive.
- It can arise externally, when the people around you make you self-conscious or point an accusatory finger at you: in childhood, "You should be ashamed," "It makes Daddy sad when you do that"; or in adulthood, "You should have studied Economics," "You shouldn't have married X," "You shouldn't have gotten involved in this business," "You should have seen it coming."

Careful! Inner voices can be just as damaging to your mind and body as those coming from outside.

Guilt demoralizes us; it allows no forward progress. Some feelings of guilt can lead to very severe mental states. It's relatively common to encounter very neurotic personalities in treatment—depressed people who have locked themselves into a cycle of guilt that they cannot manage to heal. When guilt has a basis in reality—we sometimes *do* do the wrong thing—try to use this past mistake as a motivation to improve, to learn, and to overcome.

CASE STUDY: CATALINA

Catalina got married when she was 31. She has worked all her adult life for a multinational company, traveling through Spain and Europe. She enjoys her work, and had never felt any maternal urges.

At 33, she became a mother for the first time. After the birth, during her period of maternity leave, she began to feel enormous attachment to her son, Eduardo. She surprised herself, reading insatiably about babies, breastfeeding, and motherhood. She signed up to various websites to learn and become more informed. She attended postpartum group sessions with other mothers, took her son to baby massage, and devoted herself to talking with other women about the daily development of little Eduardo.

Four months passed, and the day arrived when she was meant to return to work. She had always been someone with a lot of professional drive, but she began to experience feelings of anxiety a few days before her return. When she went back, she was incapable of disconnecting from home—she installed a system on her phone for monitoring how her baby was all day long.

When she left the house, a "horrible feeling of guilt" over abandoning her son would well up in her. This thought led to a state of high alert and distress that prevented her from performing at work. Guilty thoughts flooded through her mind, and her one desire was to get back home, embrace her son, and be with him. She realized that she was forging an unhealthy mother-son relationship. A couple of months later, she asked for leave due to anxiety.

When I see her in consultation for the first time, I realize that her guilt has developed into an anxious-depressive state. She never imagined that she could feel a maternal instinct—a very natural one, but unacknowledged by her for many years—and now still, every time the thought of work occurs, thousands of toxic voices crowd together in her head, judging and criticizing her for abandoning her son.

We begin therapy to determine the exact level of distress she's presenting. At the same time, we begin a minute examination of her inner state, her blockage and anxiety derived from guilt. We realize that she comes from a family in which the mother always worked—her parents were separated and her father lived far away—and she has never had a particularly close relationship to her. She explains: "My mother spent the day working. She left us in a neighbor's house, where we did our homework and played with the other kids. She's only kissed me or told me that she loves me a few times. She's very cold, extremely pragmatic, and she judges me very harshly when I do something wrong."

The therapy lasted a few months, until she began to accept her feelings of attachment, which had been inhibited. She learned to understand her mother, the circumstances that surrounded her childhood, and to love her as she was. Now she works reduced hours and is looking forward to having her second child.

HOW TO PACIFY FEELINGS OF GUILT

- Pay attention and take note of the main triggers of guilt that come up for you throughout the day. Observe which life events affect you most. Accept that you might be judging yourself too harshly in some situations.

- Make a list of failures, faults, and actions you feel guilty about that you have performed over the course of your life and have marked you in some way. Do this without exaggerating, being neither excessively harsh nor excessively indulgent, trying to find a middle ground. Rate them from zero to five. These scores will help you realize that you can measure your perception of guilt quite accurately.

- Observe a past event that you're tormented by as though you were sitting in a train, watching this scene from your life pass by. Acknowledge that there is no way to change the outcome now. Guilt doesn't help the situation or make you grow. It isn't constructive. It's just a toxic emotion that prevents you from moving forward and that must be processed and eliminated.

- Return to your present moment by asking this bold question: What am I losing in the present because I'm living mired in guilt? You'll be surprised—I guarantee that good things are happening all around you—you just aren't capable of seeing them.

- Learn to love yourself, and to move through life with a sense of well-being. The most important thing is knowing how to be good to yourself. People who remain stuck in a state of guilt can't manage to see their strengths or their talents. They see everything as crashing down on them because of their limitations or defects—because their perception is distorted!

- Be careful of developing a victim mentality. Guilt is a slippery slope that finishes, in many cases, in a constant state of victimhood, a neurotic and toxic behavior that obstructs your clear vision of life and your way of relating to others.

- Look for things that you like about yourself. They exist, but sometimes your state of mind or your links to the past stop you from seeing them. I'm sure that inside you there are abilities that can motivate positive growth, even if others don't like them! Your main challenge: Let go of the opinions and judgments of others.
- Focus on your values. Guilt carries the seeds of destruction of entire value systems. You don't know what to believe or why to believe it. What governs your life? Think about whether you're being hard on yourself because of something imposed from outside or because of demands that you have chosen to take on over the course of your life.

DEPRESSION

Depression is the malady of our times. It would really be more accurate to speak of *depressions* in the plural, because there are multiple types that can crop up in the clinical context. Depression currently constitutes one of the major epidemics of modern society. In my country, Spain, there are approximately 2.5 million people suffering from it.

It's a disease, and as such there are causes, symptoms, prognostics, treatments, and, in some cases, preventative measures that go with it. There are two types: endogenous depressions and exogenous depressions. Between them falls an intermediate spectrum of mixed forms of depression. In addition, there are reactive depressions, arising in response to life itself.

It is now thought that all of these types are much more intertwined than was previously believed. There are various neurological circuits and substances implicated in depression, among which the most studied are the monoaminergics—serotonin, dopamine, and norepinephrine—but it hasn't yet been demonstrated that any of these circuits present a degeneration or dysfunction that is clearly responsible for the symptomatology, as happens with Alzheimer's, Parkinson's, or other neurological diseases.

Some now postulate that the neurobiological hypothesis of depression has a relationship to neuroplasticity in the circuits charged with cognitive and emotional functions. This means we might really be talking about a disorder with the circuits rather than with the transmitters themselves.

Depression is a disease of sadness. An infinite number of negative symptoms can converge in depression: pain, dejection, apathy, loss of appetite, disillusionment, a lack of desire to live, indifference and lethargy (lacking the energy to perform any activity), suicidal ideation, disrupted sleep, and problems with attention and concentration.

Depression leaves you without the energy or the desire to do anything. Its symptoms are extremely varied and can range from the physical (headaches, chest pain, or generalized pain distributed throughout the body); to the psychological (most important, a psychological downturn, although a lack of vision for the future is also common, with everything becoming colored by negativity and feelings of guilt); the behavioral (behavioral paralysis and blockage, isolation); the cognitive (struggles with concentration and memory, dark thoughts, and ideas that deform our perception of reality and turn it against us); or the social, also known as assertive (social abilities become blurred and lost, and communication and interpersonal exchanges grow clumsy and distant). The symptomatology of depression can, in many cases, be vague and manifest as bodily symptoms; according to some studies, around 60 percent of cases initially seek medical advice for a physical symptom.

A person who hasn't experienced clinical depression doesn't know the true nature of sadness. The suffering caused by depression can become so profound that suicide seems like the only way out.

Nobody is immune from depression. It's true that there are factors that increase one's risk—family, genes, socioeconomic status—but consulting rooms are full of people from all walks of life making their way through the dark tunnel of depression: writers, athletes, musicians, actresses, singers, politicians, wealthy entrepreneurs, and extremely successful people of all stripes . . . Many among them have confessed to suffering from depression or undergoing treatment.

FAMOUS SUFFERERS FROM DEPRESSION

Vincent Van Gogh. The genius artist was a patient at a psychiatric hospital; unfortunately for him and the history of art, his condition worsened to the point where he committed suicide. The red-headed Dutch painter, with his mutilated ear, felt that his stormy life lacked meaning; professionally, he considered himself a failure, and in fact he only sold one picture in his lifetime. In the end he let himself be overcome—his last words were, "The sadness will last forever."

Michelangelo Buonarroti. In the case of the man many believe to be the greatest sculptor in history, his depression originated in what we would now call body dysmorphic disorder, that is to say an obsession with a body part one finds displeasing.

Michelangelo is said to have had an unprepossessing face, with a nose disfigured by an act of violence by one of his many jealous enemies, Pietro Torrigiano, a legendarily bad-tempered sculptor. Torrigiano worked in the court of Lorenzo de Medici, who had a great admiration for Michelangelo. One day, in a fit of envy or jealousy, he broke his nose. Michelangelo, traumatized, isolated himself and avoided the company of others for many years. His good friend, the poet Poliziano, gave him excellent therapeutic support during this period of his life.

Ernest Hemingway. He suffered a serious depression at the end of his life. He felt a profound sadness and disillusionment. In an attempt to cure himself, he underwent various rounds of electroshock therapy. At the time, this treatment was relatively new and quite rudimentary, and it gave rise to serious adverse effects in patients. Ernest lost his memory, and his cognition was severely affected. When he received the Nobel Prize in 1954, in recognition of his writing career, he said, "Writing, at its best, is a lonely life. Organizations for writers palliate the writer's loneliness but I doubt if they improve his writing."

His father had committed suicide in 1928. On learning of it, he wrote, "I'll probably go the same way."

And indeed, some years later, in 1961, his prophecy was fulfilled.

Depression in children translates into a different set of behaviors and symptoms. The depression is externalized, demonstrated through the child's conduct. A child of 10 or 12 still doesn't have enough emotional vocabulary or mastery of verbal self-expression to explain what he is feeling. This is why, to uncover possible depression in a child, we must be alert and correctly interpret his changes in behavior: he may stop playing, speak very little, turn inward, get bored, cry frequently, struggle to concentrate, and fall behind in school. Parents should be capable of looking below the surface and seeing when their children are adrift, lose motivation, or have changed their demeanour.

Fortunately, today we have the benefit of real improvements in the treatment of depression at every level, although it's true that advances in the field aren't occurring as rapidly as we might like, and we all know or have heard of someone who spends their whole life on medication. Attacking the symptoms from the get-go and finding the right treatment increase the chances of a cure. Many depressions stem from a state of permanent anxiety—I'll talk more about this later—and therefore treatment should be oriented toward reinforcing the foundations of a positive mental state: good management of stress and the emotions as well as the background personality.

A Therapeutic Example

In my consultation practice, I tend to work schematically. I try, in the simplest way, to build a model—an actual chart—of the patient's personality, reflecting their way of being, their style of stress management, and their psychological symptoms, so that the person understands what's happening to them and can work on it. Let's look at an example.

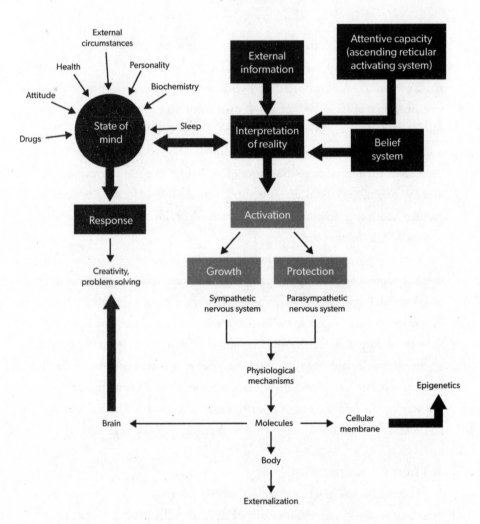

SCHEMA OF REALITY

Rojas, M. (2018)

CASE STUDY: ALEJANDRA

Alejandra comes in seeking counseling for her depression, panic attacks, and recurrent migraines. She's been undergoing pharmaceutical treatment for five years, during which she's experienced periods of improvement that last a few weeks. On analyzing her personality more deeply, we find a woman with avoidant traits—exaggerated shyness—who tends to get trapped in circular thinking and displays hypersensitivity. We look at what she sees as her stress triggers—interacting with others, working in a public-facing role, and seeing her ex (with whom she has a complicated relationship), as well as reaching the end of the month, when she always experiences financial difficulties.

In this case, it isn't simply a question of administering medication for her sadness or panic attacks but of working on the cause (her avoidant personality); on her stress management (for her, working with the public and attending social events are important factors in creating tension); on the symptoms of anxiety (I manage this with awareness and relaxation techniques); and then on the depression, which may or may not require medication.

In my experience of counseling, working with a scheme allows the patient to better understand what is happening to them and exactly how we're working on their inner state, as well as the therapeutic aim of any medication administered.

FORGIVENESS

Forgiveness is an act of love and an elevated mindset with which to approach other human beings and life in general. To forgive is to respond positively when you have been treated negatively. It's a special form of surrender, and it lifts human beings to a higher plane.

I'm not naïve—I know how difficult it is to forgive certain behaviors.

It's not the same to pardon someone after being lightly wounded as it is to forgive them after suffering in a significant and really damaging way. Disdain, unjustified aggression, humiliation, betrayal, marital infidelity, or harsh criticism can generate levels of suffering that can be difficult, or nearly impossible, to overcome.

In Cambodia, I listened to the most chilling, terrifying stories of my life. I kept notebooks of what I heard, and sometimes, reading back over them, I still end up crying all over again. I wanted to help girls who had lived or were living in prostitution, and who had suffered cruelly, but I didn't know how to help them find a way out of their pain. I've always thought that psychiatrists and psychologists help people who are suffering, wounded, or blocked to find a way out; in Cambodia, however, I didn't know how to provide that "therapy."

One day I met Mey, and she gave me a solution.

I met Mey on a hot, gray day in August. Somaly* had told me about a house in the Cambodian hills that sheltered a center for very young girls. When we arrived at the center, what I saw remained stuck in my mind's eye. The girls were all dressed the same, so as not to call out their differences: They wore a shirt and pants in a Hawaiian-type floral pattern. Somaly went toward them, sitting down in the middle of the room. Their *maman* had arrived, and the girls came running to hug her. In a few faces you could see deep sadness, their gazes lost in a cruel and painful past. The smallest girls, five or six years old, flitted about and danced around Somaly. Others, seated in the corners, stayed completely still. Somaly, with her sweet voice, began to tell them a story in her language, Khmer. Little by little, the stragglers came to sit closer to her; a change came over their countenances, and their faces grew less cold and tense.

While I was observing this scene, a girl with a mischievous smile came up to me. I introduced myself in my rudimentary Khmer, which was very

---

* Somaly Mam is a Cambodian activist I collaborated with in Cambodia. In Chapter 5, I describe how I ended up getting to know her.

basic but sufficient to start a simple conversation. She was called Mey; she was 13 and had been at the center for a few months. When she noticed my difficulty with the language, she smiled in amusement and let slip a few words in English—it was obviously going to be easier to communicate in that language than with *my* Khmer. After a short conversation, I asked if she was happy. She answered intently, "Now I am. I want to be a journalist to write stories for children so that their mothers will read to them. The stories will have to be about how parents love and take care of their children, and don't sell them into prostitution."

Mey had brought up prostitution fearlessly, without batting an eyelid. A shiver went down my back. After a few seconds of silence, I gathered my strength and asked, "Did they sell you?"

"Yes, my grandmother sold me, and I'll never understand it."

Silence . . . then she looked up and continued. "I don't have parents. My memories begin with my grandmother, who I lived with. A year ago they took me to the house of an older foreign businessman. There were a lot of us girls in the house, some cooked, others cleaned . . . One day he called me to his room, took off my clothes, and did horrible things to me that I didn't know existed. I screamed and screamed but nobody could hear me . . ."

I embraced her, to try and console her in the face of such a memory, but she didn't show any pain, seeming to remember it at a distance. She carried on. "This happened again on different days, until I realized I couldn't endure it anymore. I decided to escape, and one night I jumped the gate and ran away. I didn't know where to go, and I didn't have anywhere to go back to. I remembered that a while before, I had met an Indian man who brought rice to our neighborhood when we didn't have any food. He was a good man. I ran to the house where he lived. He was a missionary. I had never heard about Christians. He told me about his God and how he died on a cross. I wasn't brought up in any religion, but I was interested in his story and I asked, 'How did he overcome it?' His response was, 'He forgave them.' I started to attend the little chapel nearby in the mornings, and I talked to the man on the wooden cross. I asked him to help me to forgive, so

I could be free of the anguish and the rage. One day, while I was sitting on the ground, I realized that I didn't feel hate or anger anymore. I'd forgiven the foreigner. From that day my life changed."

With excitement, I realized I was getting a glimpse of a viable solution to so much pain. She continued: "The missionary was looking into the best place to take me. We finally decided to go to the police, who brought me here. A few days later I met Somaly. Now I'm happy. I have a mother and many sisters. It's essential to overcome such immense pain through forgiveness. There's no other way to achieve peace. I try to do it with my sisters [as they call each other at the center]. I love them, I listen to them . . . I'm very lucky. I'm very happy."

I spoke to Mey at length, and all in a rush. I was impressed at how the power of forgiveness had healed her deepest wounds. Over the course of the following weeks, I tried to follow the "forgiveness model" that she had shown me.

I was profoundly marked by it; I studied, I read everything I could find on the capacity to forgive, and I based the process on the idea that understanding is healing. This means that when you understand or comprehend the reasons that motivate someone to hurt you—their life history, their way of being, their envy, their internal conflicts, etc.—you manage to relieve your own suffering.

In Mey's case, where she had so much anger against her grandmother for selling her, she told me, "Faced with the desperation of having nothing, without ill will, she was looking for an easy solution, so my sisters could eat."

There are of course bad people in the world, but the majority of those who hurt you have their reasons. Sometimes even they don't know them, but if you look, if you really hunt for them, you might be surprised by the consolation you can find.

Our suffering in life can be truly painful and torturous; this is the reason we must struggle to overcome the harm that falls to our lot. When someone holds on to their hatred, when they aren't capable of recovering from the offenses and humiliations they receive, they can turn into a bitter, resentful, neurotic person. To avoid these negative consequences, even in cases where the person who provoked the trauma has no possible justification, the victim is better off "selfishly" forgiving.

The drama and traumas that flatten and destroy one person can strengthen and regenerate another, giving them the gift of a greater capacity for love.

One toxic ingredient derived from a lack of forgiveness is resentment—re-sentiment: the repetition of a feeling, and of the thoughts that go with it, in a recurrent and harmful manner. Every religion and ethical system includes forgiveness as one of its foundational principles. Buddhism considers it in depth; there are teachings from the Buddha on the human need to forgive. In Judaism, the concept of forgiveness is fundamental, and very similar to that held by Christians. To illustrate the theme, I'm going to tell a remarkable story.

What if you can't understand . . . at all?

Simon Wiesenthal was an Austrian Jew, a professional architect. After being imprisoned in five different concentration camps during World War II, he was liberated from Mauthausen by the Americans in 1944. Once he had recuperated, he began his famous work as an implacable Nazi-hunter, traveling all around the world. He managed to bring more than a thousand Nazis to justice.

In his book, *The Sunflower: On the Possibilities and Limits of Forgiveness,*[*] he relates his personal story and his ideas about the great dilemma of forgiveness.

The anecdote that stands out on the page—and in his life—is as follows. One day, in a concentration camp, a nurse asked him to follow her. He was brought to a room where a young member of the SS, Karl Seidl, 21 and dying, had a peculiar request to make of him. Karl had received a bullet

---

[*] I recommend reading this book to deepen your knowledge of suffering and of forgiveness in difficult situations.

wound, and was experiencing his death throes. Barely capable of speech and almost completely covered in bandages, he had begged the nurse to bring a Jew to him before he died, so he could speak to him. During the hours that followed, Simon stayed by the young man, who told him his life story. He needed to express who he was, recounting his childhood, and how he had ended up with the SS youth arm, committing atrocities. He revealed to Simon, all the while tightly holding his hand, one of the worst brutalities he had carried out: beating and attacking a group of Jewish families and finally burning them in a house in Dnipropetrovsk, now in Ukraine. He continued his recital, stressing the aspects that caused him the greatest pain, among them the gaze of a small boy, who tried to jump from the window but whom Karl shot. During the hours he stayed by his side, Simon didn't utter a word.

Karl's last words were: "Here I am with my guilt. In the last hours of my life, you're here with me. I don't know who you are, I only know that you're Jewish, and that's enough. I know that what I've told you is terrible; time and again I've yearned to speak of it with a Jew and to ask his forgiveness. I know I'm asking too much of you, but without your response, I can't die in peace."

Simon couldn't stand it; he walked out of the room. His book deepens his exploration of this question: "Should I have forgiven him? . . . Was my silence at the bedside of the dying Nazi right or wrong? This is a profound moral question that challenges the conscience . . . The heart of the matter is the question of forgiveness. Forgetting is something that time alone takes care of, but forgiveness is an act of volition and only the sufferer is qualified to make the decision."[*]

The situation I've described provoked, in Simon, a huge moral dilemma over guilt, the capacity to forgive, and repentance. In the second part of his book, he interviewed 53 thinkers, intellectuals, politicians, and religious leaders—Jewish, Christian, and Buddhist; witnesses of the genocides in Bosnia, Cambodia, Tibet, and China—about what they would have done

---

[*] *The Sunflower*, S. Wiesenthal.

in his place. Twenty-eight of them responded that they wouldn't have been capable of forgiving, sixteen asked whether it was possible, and nine didn't have a clear position. Of those who did opt for forgiveness, the majority were Christian and Buddhist. The position taken by the Dalai Lama, founded on his memories of the conflict in Tibet, was in support of forgiveness, but without forgetting, so that never again could similar atrocities occur.

This book, which doesn't come to any conclusion, deciding that in the end forgiveness is a matter of individual conscience, constitutes a classic work on forgiveness and reconciliation from different points of view, both religious and personal.

Forgiving doesn't mean deciding that what the other person has done is acceptable or comprehensible. At times the crime is so atrocious and inhuman that there is no way to analyze the conduct of the perpetrator and thereby get relief. In spite of everything, even in those cases, forgiveness is necessary, because the pain that the guilty party has created doesn't deserve to find a permanent home in your mind. That wound, that poison, that resentment—each could turn you into an embittered person, if you're not capable of letting it go. Forgiving relieves the pain caused, dodges resentment, and therefore opens the way to the future up to the victim, a way which, without forgiveness, would remain permanently closed. The capacity to forgive belongs solely to the victim, and doesn't depend on the repentance of whoever caused the offense. Forgiving is a way of shedding burdens, which helps us to move forward even if the damage done is terrible and the person who caused it doesn't repent. In my clinical experience, it's always worth it.

Forgiving is traveling to the past and returning safe and sound.

If we don't forgive, if we aren't capable of purifying ourselves, we can stay stuck with our rancor, hatred, and desire for revenge. Revenge means deciding that I want to hurt the other person in return, that I want them to suffer and for bad things to happen to them. Rancor means I stay wounded and bleeding, incapable of forgetting and overcoming the harm. If this happens to us, we'll find ourselves unable to recover peace and equilibrium.

How does one forgive?

- Accept what happened. Don't deny reality.
- Try to get a little perspective on what has happened. Sometimes we're minor players in a drama unfolding elsewhere, and there's nothing we could have done to intervene. Life is full of injustices and complications that we cannot control.
- Try to distance yourself from the scene in your head by using techniques such as EMDR. EMDR—Eye Movement Desensitization and Reprocessing—was discovered by Francine Shapiro in 1987. It's a psychotherapeutic technique employed to work with post-traumatic stress disorder. It integrates elements of different psychological approaches. Using bilateral stimulation by means of eye movements, sounds, or tapping, it stimulates one cerebral hemisphere at a time. EMDR has been validated by multiple scientific studies. It's useful to patients dealing with severe trauma (due to deaths, assaults, or physical or psychological abuse) or other difficult events that have created a blockage for one reason or another. I employed it in Cambodia with very satisfactory results.
- Work on your levels of self-esteem. The capacity to forgive—to overcome rage, the thirst for vengeance, or self-pity—is greater in people who have inner strength. If the person who suffers from a terrible act is capable of overcoming it and forgiving, they're demonstrating a sense of security in themselves that accompanies healthy self-esteem.
- Be optimistic. It sometimes takes time, but the simple fact of knowing that, faced with pain, you can choose to grow, that there is hope of overcoming, can act as a soothing balm on your wounds.
- Avoid practicing denial through feelings of guilt. Be wary of turning yourself into a victim! There are people who, faced with misfortune, close themselves off and avoid making progress. The consequence of

returning time and again to past incidents in order to justify ourselves only further shuts ourselves down, cutting off our vital impulse.

- Look to the future.
- We learn to forgive by being forgiven ourselves. It's a healthy exercise to look at our recent past, and our lives, to find times when others have offered us forgiveness.
- See the other person as worthy of compassion. John Paul II said, "There is no justice without forgiveness, and no forgiveness without mercy." We must try to replace the negative with powerfully positive feelings like compassion and mercy.

WHAT IS COMPASSION?

Empathy is feeling what another person feels, putting oneself in another's place. Compassion—literally "suffering together"—is a capacity that elevates whoever exercises it. You don't just understand the pain that someone else is going through—you connect to their suffering, trying to use all your personal tools to help them move forward.

Exercising compassion from the heart has amazing effects on the mind, the body, and our relationships with others. It's a way of freeing yourself from rage and hate, making space for peace and equilibrium. Obviously the capacity to empathize is different in each individual, but it can be cultivated and helps everyone in their personal and professional relationships.

Today there is a great fear of feeling other people's pain, of getting close to someone else's suffering, in case it ruins our day in one of these ways:

- By making us feel vulnerable. Encountering other people's emotions might reopen wounds from our own lives.
- If we aren't able to help, it may give rise to the frustration of feeling useless.
- By causing us the anguish of feeling too much, and obliging us to

"take the problem home." This happens occasionally with therapy, or in the case of very sensitive people: the pain being witnessed is such that one becomes excessively moved. Because of this, it's very important to know oneself and to know how far one can go when giving of oneself to others.

LIVING WITH ANXIETY FOR THE FUTURE

CASE STUDY: JOHN

John, a 35-year-old man, was working in the Twin Towers on September 11, 2001. Finding himself in the second tower when it was hit, he raced down the stairs at the speed of light, managed to get out of the building, and remained among the ruins for several hours. When he realized that he had survived a terrible attack, he looked for other survivors in the rubble. He felt death close by him while he shouted, desperately searching for traces of life among the cadavers that surrounded him.

Several of his colleagues died that day. Months later, he couldn't endure being in the dark; he had recurring nightmares from which he awoke sweating and trembling. He wasn't able to get on a plane until many years later. His mind was easily blocked, and his body tensed up at small sounds, or images and memories of that day. John required therapy for years to overcome his anxiety, his trauma, and his horrible fear.

Let's begin at the beginning: Fear is with us from the moment we're born. It's a reality that has always existed. Without fear, we would be foolish, careless creatures. The way in which we manage this emotion defines us in our development as people. Fear is, in principle, a primary defense mechanism, but it can become our number one enemy and upset our perception of life.

Titus Livius put it well when he considered the matter: "Fear always disposes us to see things as worse than they are."

A fearful person sees their environment as hostile and upsetting, making them vulnerable to everything. We shouldn't forget that the best challenges possess an element of uncertainty; nothing great can begin without a little fear.

> *Dealing with fear isn't a question of eliminating it but of acknowledging its existence and learning to manage it well.*

Fear is a key emotion, fundamental to our inner equilibrium and our survival. We must be afraid of certain things in order not to launch ourselves imprudently into all kinds of schemes and ventures. Every human being has their fears in life, including the brave and triumphant ones. The difference is that the triumphant know how to manage their fear.

Anxiety, when we give in to it, has a terrible effect on the body. Anyone who has suffered an anxiety or panic attack has experienced a terrifying reality. Even though you're conscious that you won't die of a heart attack, in the moment, your mind doesn't allow you to keep hold of that thought with any clarity. Anxiety is characterized by fear, a vague and diffuse fear, often without a clear origin, that develops into anguish and emotional blockage.

> *Courage doesn't exist in the absence of fear, but in the ability to thrive and carry on in spite of it.*

The management of emotions is fundamental to personal equilibrium. Sometimes fear is so intense that it carries out a "palace coup," taking control of our minds and monopolizing our behavior. In these cases, the vulnerability of the sufferer is huge, and any external stimulus, no matter how small, can provoke a disproportionate reaction that disturbs the body both chemically and physiologically. In an ecosystem like this, anxiety emerges, a pathological fear that blocks us and prevents us from living a normal life.

How does the brain work when faced with fear? What exactly happens with anxiety?

The fear center is found in the cerebral amygdala, which has small physical dimensions but a very large effect on our lives and behavior. The amygdala, according to recent studies, is active during gestation, from the end of pregnancy. It has a great capacity to store emotional memories and reacts depending on the emotions that arise. It processes information relative to the emotions and warns the brain and body of danger, signaling that something isn't right, activating the reaction or response of anxiety or fear. The hippocampus—fundamental to learning and memory—codifies threatening or traumatic events in the form of memories.

A REAL EXAMPLE FROM MY LIFE

I was studying for my degree in medicine. During the exam period, many of us went to the library at the Universidad Autónoma in Madrid, because it didn't close at night and there was a good ambience for studying. I had a Medical Physics exam the next day, June 13. I remember the date because it's my saint's day, and I was going to celebrate in the afternoon.

I had stayed in the library so that two friends studying engineering could help me understand some concepts I was struggling with. I left at about a quarter to one in the morning, got in my car, and headed toward the city center.

I was driving on a well-lit dual carriageway. I wasn't going especially fast but, suddenly, on a curve, I caught sight of a car heading straight toward me, driving in the opposite direction in the same lane. The approaching headlights of the car are fixed in my memory; I swerved sharply and avoided it. My heart was beating a mile a minute, and my whole body was trembling. I stopped on the hard shoulder a few miles further on and started to cry. Suddenly I heard an awful crash behind me; I looked but I couldn't see anything.

I arrived home terrified and woke up my parents. I couldn't stop crying. I prayed, thanking God I was still alive, but I couldn't manage to relax. I put the radio on to see if the sensation of panic that was still in control of my mind would fade. After a few minutes, I heard a voice saying, "There has been an accident on the Colmenar highway, a kamikaze collision between two cars. Four people have been killed." That night marked me deeply.

I didn't sleep a wink. My exam the next morning was a real disaster. I spent the afternoon visiting friends and relatives. I was really distressed. Even weeks later, if I heard braking in the street or a louder motor noise than usual, my whole body was thrown back to that moment, experiencing tachycardia, trembling, and anguish. It took me several months to get over it. Every week I took exactly the same route: I didn't want to become blocked and be incapable of using the car or taking certain roads. I'm completely over the event now, but the experience has helped me greatly in understanding blockages caused by fear or anxiety.

Here's another example to illustrate this mental circuit.

CASE STUDY: BLANCA

Blanca went one night to collect her car in an underground parking garage. She usually traveled by bus, but on this particular day she'd had various errands to run before work, and had left the car in a nearby parking garage. When she arrived, she noticed that it was poorly lit and empty, with no security guard or checkpoint. She was very tired—she'd had a difficult day containing a certain amount of conflict, and she felt weak and exhausted.

She went hurriedly to the automatic ticket machine to pay, and then she heard a noise. A man with "a nasty look about him" came up to her. At that moment she remembered something that had happened years before, when she was working in Brazil and was robbed one night. Her heart began thumping, she started to sweat, and she couldn't think clearly. She wished she were already in her car. There was no one else nearby, and fear gripped her by the throat and choked her.

What had happened in Blanca's mind? Her amygdala had put her on guard, because the parking garage at night is—at least in her memory—a risky place, and so is the person approaching her. Her memory has retained—in the hippocampus—data about her bad experience in Brazil. To these "memorized" ideas she adds more: "I won't park here again," "I won't collect the car at night-time," and "If I have to collect my car, I'll make sure I'm not alone." Recollections, anxiety, memory, physical activation—it all comes together; the hippocampus and amygdala are a key pairing in the processing of memories and in episodes of anxiety.

The majority of circumstances that activate our mind's fear response are learned: they develop according to our experience, whether direct or reported by others. That is to say, the brain codifies certain things as "fearful," and, adapting itself, when it perceives something similar to a past event, it activates the alarm system. These fearful situations can arise from past traumatic events or events that we haven't overcome or confronted appropriately.

When the brain perceives all of reality as threatening, this is because the alert system has become hyperactive. At that point we're dealing with generalized anxiety disorder, which requires a comprehensive approach, but which usually has a good prognostic; or with post-traumatic stress disorder, which arises when a terrible event has marked us, and our mind, faced with simple stimuli, discharges a disproportionate physical reaction, recalling and reliving the day of the trauma.

HIGHLY CHARGED EMOTIONAL MEMORIES

Certain events or recollections hold a potent emotional charge. This means that, when we relive them, our neuronal connections activate in such a way that the whole body is affected—trembling, tachycardia, sweating, hyperventilation—with a consequent rise in cortisol and adrenaline.

A person with an affected or damaged amygdala has serious problems detecting warning, danger, and risk.

An amygdala hijack, to use the term coined by Daniel Goleman in his book, *Emotional Intelligence*, refers to those emotional responses that arise in an abrupt and exaggerated way.

When a stimulus is received, the body's reaction is excessive and explosive. This doesn't refer to a mental problem, necessarily, but rather a past event with a huge emotional charge that blocks the sufferer, so that, faced with a current event that indirectly recalls it, the subject isn't capable of making choices or reasoning with clarity. The individual who responds in this way finds themselves overtaken by their emotions.

We all know people who have been through this. These are people with short tempers: faced with minor stimuli, the repercussion for others is a head-on collision. You might talk about someone "blowing his top," or say "He doesn't have a filter," or "He's got a short fuse." Is there a solution? There is, in learning to manage the emotions and working on understanding the origins of these abrupt reactions.

CASE STUDY: GUILLERMO

Guillermo has been married to Laura for three years. He works in a laboratory, and she's a cardiologist. They met at a medical conference in Atlanta. She almost always came to conventions with her partner at the time, another doctor at the same hospital, but on this occasion he hadn't been able to accompany her.

Guillermo had already interacted with Laura a few times through work. She struck him as an attractive woman and he liked spending time with her. He was aware that she had a partner, a doctor that he'd seen on professional matters at times, and because of this he kept his distance. During the conference, he perceived a change in Laura—she was friendlier and more intimate and he noted that she tried to make more time for him. Guillermo, nervous, didn't know how to act, but one night, after having a few drinks together after dinner, they ended up in her room.

Guillermo, feeling awkward, wanted to know what Laura was feeling, what would happen with her boyfriend—too many questions. Guillermo was passionate and impatient—he needed to resolve his sentimental dilemma. She explained that her relationship to the other man was over, and she was going to break up with him when she got back. And she did. A few months later, Guillermo and Laura got together officially, but he was very jealous and couldn't stand for her to attend conferences alone. If anyone so much as came near her or invited her to a meal to discuss work, he would have an explosive, disproportionate reaction that was difficult to control. His excuse was always: "It happened with me, it could happen with someone else."

Guillermo was suffering an amygdala hijack around this issue.

Stimulus → immediate and disproportionate explosive reaction → inability to deal with reality → paralysis, blockage, or aggression/being blinded by emotions → repentance or forgiveness (in the best-case scenario).

HOW TO DEAL WITH AN AMYGDALA HIJACK

We've seen how this circuit works. Now let's look for a solution. Imagine that we're "mental electricians": The easiest thing would be to short-circuit the problem. Let's see how.

1. Analyze it

   What stimulus triggers you? Understanding yourself is key in these cases. Aim fearlessly for the heart of what's causing it. Is it a person, a look, a situation, perceiving something threatening? It could be the sight of blood, a conversation about a divisive issue, a thought that crosses your mind, the actions of someone around you, someone saying "no" to something you were excited about . . . The point of origin might be anything, but you need to understand what it is.

2. **What's happening in your body?**

    You'll notice that the hijack is accompanied by physical symptoms. Try to focus on how your body feels just before—how you feel physically in the instants before the emotional explosion—and on the physical signs that arise in your body during the process—tachycardia, hypertension, temperature increase, etc.

3. **Think about someone you know and admire**

    How do they react in similar situations? What is the worst version of them, when frustrated or angry? Having a model to look to for reference in difficult moments is a great help.

4. **Short-circuit that explosive connection!**

    This can be complicated; sometimes we have very elaborate and deeply embedded reaction systems that prevent us from exercising control. Being aware of it is already a sign of progress. If you manage to realize what's happening and put a brake on the cascade that you're about to initiate, even if only for a moment or a few seconds, you've gained something. In that little space of time, try to breathe deeply, sending a positive message to your mind: "You can do it!" or "Keep going!" The mind needs approximately one to two minutes to remove the blockage from a toxic emotional state, so any victory, no matter how small, brings you closer to triumph.

5. **Ask for forgiveness**

    In those moments of lost control, we have bad reactions and say things we don't mean. The vast majority of people repent their reactions and comments after the fact. Have the humility necessary to say you're sorry, and try to repair any damage you've caused. Forgive yourself as well—you may be thinking of your reaction as another failure, and it doesn't do any good to shroud yourself in feelings of guilt. Get over it. Tell yourself you'll do better next time, and find the tools that will let you.

CASE STUDY: GUSTAVO

Gustavo comes to see me because, two days previously, on his way back from a meeting in London, just after getting on the flight home to Spain, he began to notice tightness in his chest and experience shortness of breath, along with a feeling that he was losing control of himself. He tried to implement relaxation techniques on the plane, while a stewardess offered him herbal tea and attempted to calm him down.

Staying on the plane was unbearable, and he felt an urgent need to get off at any price. In spite of this, he endured the two painful hours of the flight, and after landing, nauseated and distressed, he showed up at emergency services, where they explained that he had suffered a panic attack and that he should see a psychiatrist and get medication.

Once in my consulting room, he tells me that he doesn't understand what could have happened. He recognizes that he's stressed, but what happened on the plane had never occurred before, and he describes it as the worst time of his life. He also tells me that for the past year he's traveled almost every day of the week for work. He barely has time to see his partner between journeys and meetings. He sleeps very little because of jet lag, and all of this is making him more nervous and irritable by the day. Gustavo puts the spotlight on what happened on the plane; he doesn't want it to happen to him again. I explain that he's under too much stress, that being constantly on alert has resulted in an alteration of his survival system, which has raised the cortisol levels in his body to help him overcome the demanding situations that he confronts every day.

Gustavo describes being constantly nervous and says he's beginning to have lapses of memory. Occasionally he notices his fingers and hands falling asleep, along with tachycardia and shortness of breath. I explain that he's reached a crisis point, that he suffered a panic attack on the plane and that his brain is currently in a vulnerable state; because of this he may experience another attack if he carries on in the same fashion. I emphasize that he has to learn to lower his frantic level of activity, and that the first step is to recover the restorative capacity to sleep. He has to find a way to disconnect his brain from his hectic level of activity, because he's locked in a toxic cycle that could break down again at any moment.

In addition, I give him guidelines for avoiding a crisis on the plane. Before boarding, he must try to relax, through a series of positive cognitive cues and breathing techniques. He should also carry a supply of a certain medication with him in case of emergency. The effect of this pill is almost immediate—it will act in a very short time, should he start to suffer another attack.

Many people feel secure enough, by merely keeping the medication I've described with them, to overcome a panic attack without needing to take it; they postpone taking the pill, strengthened by the conviction that as a last resort it will help them over the attack, which eventually allows them to control their attacks without pharmaceutical aid. I prescribe another medication to unblock, little by little, Gustavo's accumulated cerebral tension.

In psychotherapy, I work in depth on the origins of his level of anxiety: he's constantly on high alert, with no time to relax. He doesn't allow himself any mistakes, he doesn't rest, he eats badly—all of which has provoked his brain into a collapse, reining him in through a panic attack. A panic attack is what I sometimes call a "mental fever." That is to say, in the same way that a fever is an indication that something isn't working well in the body, a crisis of anxiety or panic tells you that something isn't right in your mind, leading finally to a collapse. In therapy I teach Gustavo to relax, to take things in a calmer way, to know how to let things go, how to make his boss see that he needs support with his tasks, and how to delegate some of his responsibilities. All of this has the aim of alleviating his excessively heavy workload.

Little by little, Gustavo begins to feel better. At the beginning, his fear of flying persists, but I don't force it because it's a secondary issue—we can postpone the goal of overcoming it until he's doing better. With time, he begins to take short flights, of about an hour or ninety minutes, which he prepares himself for with positive cognitive messages, remembering that he's carrying emergency medication, and using relaxation and breathing control techniques. Using these methods, and with the security that carrying the emergency medication gives him (he's only needed to go so far as taking it twice, in a year of treatment), Gustavo is doing much better; he can now take a plane without too many complications, and his body is slowly recovering its equilibrium.

*If a person lives in a constant state of high alert,
it produces an interpretation of reality that
makes it seem worse than it is. Your internal
responses to events treat them like real threats.
The brain's responses become confused.*

Controlling the breathing,[*] with eyes closed, while paying attention to every sensation in the body, is one of the most effective methods for stimulating the function of the parasympathetic nervous system. This, as we've already seen, regulates our internal equilibrium, or homeostasis, activates the organs that maintain the body in periods of calm—like the salivary glands, stomach, pancreas, or bladder—and inhibits those that prepare the body for emergencies or periods of tension—like the pupils, heart, or lungs.

When we manage to keep our attention fixed on our breathing, in the present, in the here and now, putting aside any thoughts that direct us toward the past or the future, each breath brings us closer and closer to relaxation, and we are able to recover our lost serenity and confidence.

Here are a few simple keys to confronting your fears and anxiety:

---

[*] This consists of interested observation of the slow, harmonic movements of inhalation and exhalation—the lifting and sinking of the abdomen and thorax, and the coming and going of air through the nostrils. I explain the technique in more detail in Chapter 6.

- Learn to recognize what these are. Be conscious. Don't hide or suppress them; every repressed emotion finds its way in again through the back door and can become the starting point for deep wounds and physical and psychological suffering.
- You overcome fear by feeling it and taking a step forward. It is vanquished by change.
- I can't say it enough: don't hesitate to go back to the beginning to untangle the starting point and cause of your insecurities—but be wary of "impossible therapies" that end up harming you more than they help.
- Try to understand your fears—you'll be able to confront and overcome them better. If we understand something, we know how to face it, and our fear diminishes.
- Fear will always exist; learn to be an optimist and find a way out of the painful cycle of thoughts that is blocking you. Don't forget that fear is a terrible liar—it always paints reality as worse than it is.
- Trust yourself. The way in which you project yourself has the power to set the best version of your brain free. Having confidence in yourself and getting excited about achieving your goals activates your creativity, your problem-solving abilities, and a more enthusiastic view of life.
- Improve your attention span. We'll talk about this more deeply in Chapter 5, along with the Ascending Reticular Activating System. Fear and anxiety become chronic when one lacks the ability to focus one's attention correctly.
- Teach your inner voice to be polite. It should be there to get you excited, not to bring you down or be a negative influence! Avoid toxic thoughts that seek to carry you once more into a crisis of anxiety or magnify your fears.
- Take care of your nutrition. For example, hypoglycemic episodes can profoundly upset you and activate your fear. Try to avoid caffeine and alcohol.

• Rest. A lack of sleep makes us more vulnerable to our fears and makes us interpret reality as more threatening than it actually is.

We become our thoughts.* Fear is inevitable, but the suffering it produces is optional. Our fears can be cured by learning to enjoy life, looking to the future with excitement, and living in the present in a balanced, compassionate way.

---

* And we become what we love! But this chapter is focused on thoughts.

5

LIVING IN THE PRESENT MOMENT

Happiness doesn't lie in what happens to us, but in how we *interpret* what happens to us. It depends on the way we assimilate reality; our capacity to orient or focus that assimilation is key to our ability to be happy. What we're going to talk about here, then, is your capacity to choose happiness instead of unhappiness. From the beginning of this book, we've discussed pain, suffering, trauma, and deep wounds. We aren't here to deny reality—we'll talk about tolerating frustration further on—but to learn to enjoy as much as possible, in spite of . . . life's spitefulness.

Your reality depends on the way you decide to perceive it.

I understand that you might find this message surprising, and a thousand sentences—barriers, resistance!—are bubbling up inside you, of the following variety: "I've already tried everything," "My life is very hard," "Everything depends on circumstance," "My childhood was terrible," "Easier said than done" . . . If you reject the possibility of choosing to cling to the good in your life—however little of it there is—you're declaring yourself vanquished in the most decisive battle of your existence.

Happiness isn't an accumulation of joys, pleasures, and positive emotions. It's much more; it also depends on having successfully overcome wounds and hardships and continuing to grow. It means living with a certain gusto despite pain and suffering, which are, to a greater or lesser degree, inevitable.

If we negate or constantly block suffering, our mind loses the knowledge of how to confront and overcome it. This doesn't mean visiting the mental equivalent of a "bad neighborhood" and trying to wage each and every battle that's offered to us, but learning to manage difficult moments. I know a lot of people who don't know how to face conflict or negative emotion, and who deny them automatically and unconsciously as a means of escape. This approach is risky; constantly avoiding the negative means cutting off part of your life and often leads to a disconnection from the suffering of those around you. We discussed the importance of compassion in the last chapter, as well as connecting in a healthy way with the suffering of others in order to help them move forward.

Let's not forget that a big mistake people often make is aspiring to an excessive degree of happiness, a constant, utopian state of joy and pleasure. This turns people into frustrated beings, permanently dissatisfied. Is happiness a person's greatest aspiration? It seems so; and happiness *can* be instantly gratifying—eating good food, seeing friends, taking a trip—but it also has a more structural component, resting on the fundamental pillars of life: family, relationship, work, culture, friends. The happiness of gratification is like a fleeting spark, while structural happiness is a symptom of a balanced life.

I'm going to communicate various practical ideas to you here. You've probably read many of them or even experienced them at some point in your life. I've brought together everything my father taught me—I've been learning by his side for more than 30 years—along with the numerous books, articles, and studies I've read,[*] and, above all, what I've observed

---

[*] I recommend many of these in the bibliography.

of the inner life of the many people I've accompanied through their worst moments and their recovery. My intention is that what you read on this theme will be useful to you in your life, as you try to help those around you.

The reality of your life depends on how you decide to respond or react to certain circumstances, that is to say the behavior that arises in the face of external stimuli. Here I want to communicate another important idea.

Every emotion is preceded by a thought.

The mind is responsible for generating emotions. A feeling is the physical reaction to an emotion. Without the brain, there are no emotions. In cases of brain injury, stroke, or malformation, areas of the brain can be affected in such a way that a person no longer "feels." Someone can lose the feeling in their extremities—and get burned when they don't react!—if this area of their brain is deactivated or injured.

Beginning a few years ago, through looking at people who have lost their speech after a cerebral infarction (or stroke), much has been discovered about the areas of the brain in charge of this function. This was the starting point of cerebral mapping. We now have tools that allow us to examine the functioning of the brain in real time, which in turn allows us to carry out direct observations of how certain areas react and are altered when someone carries out an activity or experiences a stimulus. One of these techniques is functional magnetic resonance. This is used for clinical treatment as well as for research. The technique allows us to detect changes in the distribution of blood flow from moment to moment, thereby permitting us to understand the mind and the nervous system in a much deeper, more comprehensive way, without the need for more aggressive approaches, such as opening up the brain or waiting for an autopsy. This advanced neuroimaging technique gives us the opportunity to observe how our brains are activated by certain thoughts, motivations, or states of anxiety or depression.

A FUNDAMENTAL DISCOVERY

Every thought generates a mental and physiological change. I emphasize this idea at various points in the book. Don't forget this, because if you are one of those who suffer, who lose control of themselves, or who want to understand themselves better, understanding this process is going to help you a lot.

From a very young age, we must reckon with ideas about ourselves that may be self-imposed or assimilated from outside, such as: "I'm impulsive," "I've always been this way," "My father was the same," "I'm nervous," "I hate crowds," or "I'm afraid of flying." These sentences about yourself function in practice as mental barriers that prevent you from progressing freely in these areas. I say "sentences" because they have a blocking effect on you, as if they were condemnations passed down from on high.

Harmful emotions are caused by thoughts, whether conscious or not. And thoughts can be learned or reeducated. To successfully become a happy person, fulfilled and at peace, you must work on the way you think. If you do, you'll be surprised by the results.

You change your reality when you
change the way you think!

Make a thorough examination of the ideas you have about yourself or the ones that come up in dark moments of sadness or anguish. That toxic emotion arises because something crosses your mind and then enters you in a harmful way.

This isn't easy. You'll be dealing with what I call "automatisms": reactions that arise involuntarily because you've spent your life performing them when triggered by certain stimuli or thoughts. It's complicated to untangle yourself from the "should haves" that have attached themselves to your behavior over time. To modify toxic thoughts, or one's belief system—one's way of processing information—one must pay attention to which thoughts are acting as limits or barriers.

A belief system isn't necessarily bad, and indeed in many cases it may be good. For example, if every time you see the sun come out, you feel joy and you think that today you'll give a little bit extra because the sun grants energy to your body, your belief system is helping you; if, on the other hand, you see gray skies or it starts to rain and you say, "Today is going to be horrible," your belief system is limiting you. This can happen with external events or internal ideas and sensations. If you arrive at a dinner with friends and something hits you the wrong way or makes you feel uncomfortable, there's probably something there that has unconsciously recalled a negative past experience—the food, a person, everyone's positions around the table, a smell, or something similar.

We can train the mind and regulate our emotions. Think, for example, about riding a bike. When you get on a bike for the first time, in general you use training wheels to avoid falling. As you shed your fear, you dare to go faster, to go downhill, or even to take a hand off the handlebars. One day, you take off the extra wheels and you struggle to balance. You think you won't be able to do it, that you'll fall—and maybe you do!—but, suddenly, you've got it. Months or years might pass, but next time you get on a bicycle, you'll still have the knack; there's no need to put the training wheels back on, because your "mind" already knows how to balance.

Something similar happens when training your thoughts. As you'd expect, it's not quite such a simple process, but mental practice has an extraordinary effect on the way in which we perceive reality. If, every time you ride a bike or drive a car or ski, you only think about the times you fell, had an accident, or injured yourself, you'll end up avoiding those activities, because of the mental strain they put you through. This is how a thought becomes a limiting certainty, when you double down on it and it becomes an excuse to avoid something. Your mind has been fabricating automatisms all your life that lead to useless blockages around certain challenges or goals that arise before you.

This is why I'm talking about making a decision! Take control of yourself, and avoid throwing blame elsewhere, on the toxic people around you or on your social or financial circumstances.

Let go of the role of victim; start being
the hero of your own life story.

Here I want to present a chart that may help you to understand your way of being and feeling in the present moment.

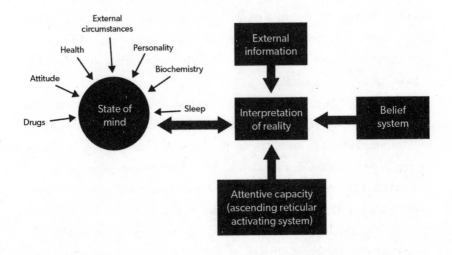

After receiving an external signal, we react and interpret reality according to three factors:

- Our belief system
- Our state of mind
- Our capacity for paying attention to and perceiving reality

After this interpretation is made, the body will respond by going into one of two modes: alert or protective, calling on the sympathetic and parasympathetic nervous systems, respectively, and thereby affecting both mind and physiology.

Let's analyze each of these factors in detail, beginning with the belief system.

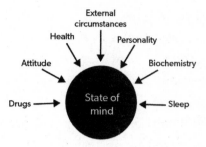

BELIEF SYSTEM

What makes a belief system? Your belief system is based on your preconceptions about how to look at life and the world around you, as well as what you believe about yourself—whether because you've arrived at a conclusion all on your own or because as a child or adult it's been repeated to you over and over: "I'm like this," "I've always struggled to wake up," "I don't get along well with people," "I'm afraid of flying," "I'm not good at sports," and so on.

These beliefs are opinions we have about the different aspects of life. They're intimately linked to the way in which we interpret the world and can be both conscious—"I realize I think this"—or unconscious, having been there all our lives.

A belief system includes values, which color our way of feeling, acting, and reacting. Beliefs continue to form throughout our lives, translating the personalized, specific vision that each of us has of life. Sometimes adolescents smoke and drink at an early age because they feel more "adult." There are other factors that can influence people to begin drinking, but one very common cause is insecurity, and the fact that drinking makes them feel more socially accepted. Even knowing that it's bad for their health and that it can be profoundly damaging, their unconscious beliefs about themselves eclipse the rational risks that they know alcohol and tobacco use entail.

Why Is This So Important to Think About?

Our belief system predisposes us to expect certain things in life and holds a potent influence over us. It supplies us with ready-made arguments for acting one way or another. These judgments are deeply rooted in our minds and never questioned; they can be decisive, in the sense that we build our interpretation of reality and our reactions to it on this foundation. These beliefs are universal: we have them about the world in general, about others, about ourselves, about concepts, about ideologies . . .

When things *never* turn out as we hope or we're *always* suffering because of our surroundings, or if we feel radically maladapted, perhaps we should first analyze our vision of the world, or how our belief system is constructed. We may find that our beliefs are limiting our inner growth. Don't be afraid to question what's limiting you, because it may lead to an improved capacity to perceive reality and focus on your Best Possible Self (BPS).*

Some of these beliefs form serious obstacles to our ability to achieve our goals or confront challenges in a healthy way, because they block our minds with feelings of insecurity and fear.

Let's continue.

STATE OF MIND

Happiness—as I've been saying throughout these pages—doesn't depend on reality itself but on how I interpret that reality. Here, my state of mind has a significant impact. I'll give you a common example: you're happy because your team won the Champions League; if you see your boss, with whom you have a bad relationship, the next day and he supports the same team, you'll probably look at him with a less critical gaze and be capable of carrying on an amicable, enjoyable conversation with him. If, on the other hand your team loses, and your brother, a fan of the rival team that won,

---

* In Chapter 9, I'll expand on my ideas for bringing out your Best Possible Self.

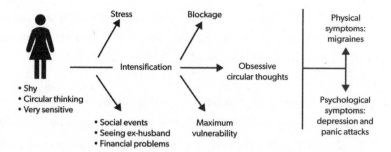

calls you to talk about the defeat, you might not even answer the phone, instead just switching it off and going to bed with no supper.

So what does our state of mind depend on?

There are different factors that modulate and change our state of mind. There isn't room here to go into excessive detail, and you could write a whole book just on this specific topic. But let's explore the basics.

1. **Drug and alcohol consumption**

   Consuming these substances is seriously harmful to mental health. One of their principal effects is a grave alteration in the perception of sensations and stimuli. We all know people who, after ingesting alcohol, become more sensitive and vulnerable, around whom we need to take care with our reactions and comments. Frequent consumption of or addiction to these substances profoundly alters the state of mind and interpretation of reality of those who consume them.

2. **Biochemistry or genetics**

   There are people who are more prone to depression or breakdown, due to genetic factors or having previously suffered severe illnesses like bipolar disorder, recurring depression, or generalized anxiety. Hormonal states also have an influence, creating special vulnerability in women—premenstrual tension, postpartum depression, and so on. It's likely that people who come from families where various members have depression possess a more fragile mental state and are more sensitive to external events.

3. **Physical health and external circumstances**

   If we're going through a difficult period professionally or experiencing a significant physical ailment, this will influence the way in which we perceive reality, because our state of mind will be rendered more sensitive and vulnerable. When we fall ill, or a difficult time or extreme situation arises in our lives, being conscious that we aren't perfectly objective can help us not to be so hard on those around us.

4. **Personality type**

   This section touches on everything from severe personality disorders (borderline, avoidant, schizoid) to marked personality traits that have a profound influence on mental states. For example, young people with borderline personality disorder—defined by impulsivity, emotional instability, intense fear of abandonment, self-harm, and low tolerance of frustration—suffer intense emotional highs and lows, put radical interpretations on reality, and perceive their environment as continually threatening. All of this means that, far from acting rationally, their reactions are often guided by aggression and rage. Getting them to a point where they can enjoy life and maintain internal equilibrium requires them to do significant work on their personalities, using methods from pharmacotherapy to individual or group psychotherapy. Another personality type that is prone to suffering is known as the HSP: highly sensitive person. This type can't currently be found in DSM-5—the manual of mental disorders—but it exists and has important consequences for those who fall in this category.

CASE STUDY: ERNESTO

Ernesto is a patient who comes to see me about his anxiety. He began having episodes at university, around his exams, but now he suffers them in a multitude of places and situations. To this he adds his acknowledgment that he is a "depressive" person. He elaborates: "For no apparent reason, I'll be somewhere and need to get out of there, I get nervous and can't enjoy myself."

He runs a few men's clothing shops, a family business where he works with his wife. He has two small children. He describes himself as someone who tends to get sad easily. He admits to having lots of mood swings he can't explain. I ask him, after our first session, to take note of his worst moments in order to analyze the causes of his daily emotional crashes. When he next comes to my office, he comments, "You're going to think I'm worse than I am."

I smile. It's a phrase I hear very often in the consulting room, when someone is ashamed to tell me about some mania or strange thought. He explains that after many years he's realized that the décor of the places he visits and the way people are dressed have a profound effect on his mood. He describes in meticulous detail how one day at the house of his parents-in-law he saw that the wall paint was flaking, and in that moment he felt he "had to get out of there; I just couldn't stand it." He indicates that if the places he spends time aren't well cared for, they give off "something bad, and I get blocked." He adds that this also happens to him with clothing, noises and smells. "I need people to take care of the details and be well-mannered; if they aren't, I don't want to go there or see them again. I don't enjoy it."

He adds that, if he's eating dinner out with his wife and he doesn't like her shoes or her dress, "I'm incapable of being affectionate, I become surly and want to go home as soon as possible."

He remarks that he startles easily at loud noises or dissonant stimuli. In Ernesto, I see a person who's so sensitive that he's actually raw. What Ernesto is suffering from is known as the HSP personality—Highly Sensitive Person.

WHAT DEFINES AN HSP: HIGHLY SENSITIVE PERSON

Do you notice that you worry about other people more than normal? Are you constantly looking for tranquillity and calm? Are you upset by chaotic environments? Do you have a more intuitive understanding of reality than the people around you?

These are some of the traits of people described as HSPs, individuals whose nervous systems are more sensitive, and who perceive changes and details in their environment more intensely. Excessive stimulation is profoundly upsetting for them. This personality type has probably existed throughout history but has only recently become known or been studied at all. It may also be that it's becoming more common, given that we now live in the most overstimulated society in history and, therefore, it's easier for certain people's senses to become saturated.

These people are particularly intuitive, but poor control of their emotions or a lack of awareness of their issues can lead them to become overwhelmed and emotionally blocked.

To list a few of their characteristics:

- They feel things with greater intensity.
- They intuitively pick up on the smallest details of their surroundings. They have great observational capacity: they notice everything about a room, clothing, art, the weather, or others' moods.
- They feel tired and overwhelmed by excessive stimuli more easily.
- They have enormous empathy and are capable of putting themselves in others' shoes, worrying a lot about those around them. They're easily moved.
- Many of these individuals have a certain degree of shyness.
- They tend to be more reflective and cautious than other people when confronting a situation or a challenge. They need a lot of security before making a decision or launching themselves into a project; because of this, they tend to gather a lot of data beforehand and only decide after meticulous analysis.

- They process information with a lot of subtlety and depth; they're often perfectionists, given the great value they place on details.
- They value etiquette highly and are very conscientious about their behavior.
- They're more sensitive to criticism; it costs them a lot to accept the negative things that others say.
- They're intensely affected by minor details, sounds, smells, or changes in temperature.
- It's as common for men as for women to be highly sensitive, although it may seem more frequent in women. The truth is, this set of symptoms has increased among men in recent years, and they often don't know how to deal with the feelings it brings up.
- Some individuals develop more frequent bouts of anxiety or depression, due to their increased vulnerability to both internal and external worlds.

These individuals must learn to adapt, and be aware of places that trigger them more, or the types of people or environments that tend to block them. In the case of children with this personality type, one must learn how to treat them without tipping into overprotectiveness, by understanding their disproportionate reactions to certain situations.

5. Sleep

This section has special importance. We spend—or at least we should—a third of our lives in the arms of Morpheus. Sleep is important, and we should care for it accordingly.

Let's take a look at the night-time world of sleep. We all know what it's like to toss and turn all night without getting any sleep, or falling asleep but waking up multiple times. In both cases one gets up in the morning with a feeling of exhaustion. Without enough sleep, the mind doesn't function normally. Problems with learning and memory arise, along with difficulty paying attention and various cognitive mistakes. A lack of rest or insufficient rest turn us into sensitive, irritable creatures who can't respond adequately to external stimuli.

A lack of sleep also affects the immune system: the parasympathetic nervous system, in charge of rest, recuperation, and manufacturing lymphocytes, becomes weakened and profoundly imbalanced.

Nightmares, waking up in the night, sleeping lightly, or a feeling of not having rested are some of the chief reasons that people seek medical, neurological, or psychiatric help. At some points in life medication may be necessary, but chronic use of pharmaceuticals has harmful effects on the brain. The first long-term studies of the consequences of abusing pharmaceuticals in order to sleep are now becoming available. Benzodiazepines—alprazolam, lorazepam, diazepam, and other derivatives—introduced into the body will induce sleep, each according to its particular mechanism, but sustained use over time will lead to tolerance, abuse, and dependence. Withdrawal is, in the majority of cases, a problem.

Sleep is fundamental because it's the basis for repairing certain areas of the brain, among them the hippocampus—the key to memory and learning, which regulates fear at various levels. During the night our memory reconstructs itself, and what has been learned in the day is relived. This is why students who sleep badly get worse exam results. Be careful of burning the midnight oil, staying up all night, and fueling a marathon study session with caffeine! Perhaps the next day you'll get through the test, but your brain will not have consolidated what it learned at night; it will simply have drawn on short-term memory to get through the immediate challenge.

During sleep, emotions are also stored, whether they are appreciative ones or feelings of resentment and rage. This is why it's so important to practice bringing joyful or positive thoughts to mind before going to bed.

JUST CURIOUS, WHY DOES COFFEE KEEP YOU AWAKE?

Strange, but very interesting. Let's see. Any activity we carry out—working, studying, practicing a sport, moving around—requires the use of energy. What is our physical energy called? Its name is ATP—adenosine triphosphate. Each cell nourishes itself on molecules of this substance, principally furnished by what we eat. When we engage in exercise, work, study, or thought, we make use of ATP, which the body consumes little by little.

Every time we use an ATP molecule, it's broken up and divided: it can shed up to three molecules of phosphate, leaving one of adenosine. This adenosine molecule is important for rest, because it brings on sleep. The brain contains sensitive receptors, specialized for adenosine. If levels of the molecule are elevated, our body perceives a feeling of sleepiness, and our sleep will be deeper. The body—which is very wise—uses this system to generate a sensation of tiredness and induce sleep after exertion, exercise, and study. There are other molecules responsible for the process of repose, but elevated levels of adenosine have huge repercussions on sleep and help us experience better rest.

What role does coffee play? This is where caffeine enters the picture: the anti-sleep molecule par excellence. It was discovered by the German chemist Friedlieb Ferdinand Runge in 1819.

It has a strong resemblance to adenosine and is what we call a non-selective antagonist to adenosine receptors; this means that consuming caffeine blocks the brain receptors sensitive to adenosine. At that point the brain is no longer receiving the signal that it's tired, and so it can stay awake longer, working or carrying out other activities.

Getting too little sleep has damaging effects on both body and mind. A human being generally needs four or five sleep cycles a night, each of which last about 90 minutes.

Here's an example, which I'm sure has happened to you at some point. You wake up in the middle of the night, feeling wide awake. You manage to go back to sleep, and then when your alarm goes off and you get up in the morning, you feel befuddled and tired. Why? It's related to sleep cycles.

There are five phases: phases 1 and 2 are light sleep, phases 3 and 4 are deep sleep, and phase 5, the REM (rapid eye movement) phase, is where we have dreams. Every cycle lasts, as we've said, about 90 minutes: 60 to 65 minutes in phases 1 to 4, plus 20 minutes in phase 5. Sleep scientists currently maintain that good sleep depends less on the number of hours spent in bed than on the number of sleep cycles achieved.

Here's something to try, especially if your sleep phases are regular. Choose a time to get up; measure in 90-minute intervals to coincide with the approximate length of a sleep cycle, so first 90 minutes, then three hours, four and a half hours, six hours, seven and a half hours, and so on. The time you choose depends on whether you need to get up early for a flight or to get something done in the morning, or if you're learning to manage your sleep. Let's look at an example: If you go to bed at 12 a.m. and set the alarm for 7:30 a.m., it will be less effort to wake up, and you might even notice that your brain activates more easily and is more refreshed. If you set it for 8 a.m., even though you're sleeping more, oddly enough you'll need to make a greater effort to get out of bed. Your alarm clock will have gone off in the middle of a phase of deep sleep.

Each person is different, and sleep cycles may be affected by factors like exercise, stress, medication, or alcohol. We all know someone who sleeps less than five hours a night and yet can function and seems perfectly able to work. Every individual's sleep cycles, therefore, deserve particular study, in order to adapt our schedules to our personal needs.

Sleep Hygiene: Five Tips for Sleeping Well

Avoid using electronic devices before sleeping: Be careful with screens, video games, social media, and the like before putting yourself to bed. There have been various studies indicating that light from a screen—whether it's your phone, a tablet, or a television—has a harmful effect when you absorb it before going to bed. A study published in 2014 in the *British Medical Journal* carried out on 9,846 adolescents aged between 16 and 19 demonstrated that the use of a screen disrupted their normal patterns of sleep. The more you use a device before sleeping, the greater the risk of inadequate rest. The problem is rooted in sleep onset latency (SOL): the time needed to actually fall asleep. The blue light of a screen blocks the secretion of the sleep hormone, melatonin. Studies confirm that this light diminishes production of this substance by up to 22 percent. Some devices have a nighttime mode, in which the light emitted by the screen is filtered and has a much weaker effect on melatonin.

Be careful with emotional stimulation: A worrying conversation, a dinner that ends in an argument, a heated discussion with your partner—these are the ingredients of a bad night's rest. If you see a terrifying film or hear upsetting news, your mind will go over and over the last thing you saw when you go to bed.

Each person is different when it comes to sleep. There are people who can fall asleep in the middle of an action movie, and others who can't get any sleep, tortured by stimuli so small as to be imperceptible to the rest of us. The important thing is to know yourself and accept that there are points in your life when you're more vulnerable. In order not to decrease the quality of your rest, you may have to pay more attention to the emotions that are impacting your sleep.

Choose the last thought of the day carefully: Be wary of mentally going over everything that's worrying you once you're in bed, and try not to dwell on all the bad things that happened during the day, or might happen tomorrow. Focus on something joyful and positive that happened to you or brought a smile to your face. However bad the day has been, there's always something positive to hold onto.

Adopt a healthy routine: Sleep hygiene relies on the brain's ability to prepare itself to enter the phases of sleep in a healthy way. It's recommended to the parents of newborns that they develop a "ritual" for putting their babies to bed, so that the babies' brains become conditioned to sleep. Something similar happens in adults. A shower, reading something calming, drinking an herbal tea, mediating or praying, listening to music, or watching a series that helps you to disconnect—all of these can be "rituals" for preparing your mind to dive into the depths of sleep.

TWO FRIENDS—OR ENEMIES

Be careful about doing too much exercise at night. Just as it can help some people to release cortisol and achieve a more profound rest, it can be activating for others, and prevent them from sleeping.

Large dinners and alcohol are disruptive agents for sleep. Be careful with caffeine, tea, and other stimulants before sleeping.

Sleep in the dark: This might surprise you. Many people take advantage of summer weather to sleep with the window open and wake up when the first rays of sunshine enter the room. This isn't a problem, as long as you don't mind getting up early. What I'm referring to here is keeping a light on in your room, from the television's standby light to notifications that illuminate your phone's screen, or a light in the hall. However small and imperceptible these lights seem, they have a harmful effect on melatonin production.

Mood depends on attitude: The attitude you bring to any situation determines how you will respond to it. A job interview, a date, a test—the outcomes of all of these are influenced by the way I approach them. There are people who prefer always to "expect the worst" in order not to be disappointed. It's true that, thinking like this, you might be pleasantly surprised by the unexpected; but we know that the brain is ignited by placing a positive attitude at the center of your behavior.

My attitude is the decision I make about how to confront life. Because it's a decision, I can always work on and improve it.

Attitude is a powerful activator of mood. There are times when one finds oneself in a depressive state that doesn't respond to any attitude, but we know that if a person who is suffering, ill, and experiencing pain deploys their best mindset—even if it's a huge effort—things shift and improve little by little.

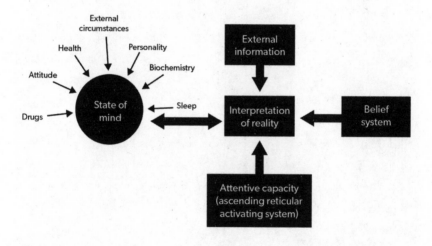

ATTENTIVE CAPACITY: THE ASCENDING RETICULAR ACTIVATING SYSTEM (ARAS)

The true act of discovery does not consist of going out to seek new countries, but in learning to see the old country with new eyes.

—Marcel Proust

The ascending reticular activating system has an ugly name, but it is honestly an interesting and inspiring part of the brain.

THE DAY MY LIFE CHANGED: MEETING SOMALY MAM

I had finished my degree in medicine. I was undergoing the official examination in order to be able to choose my specialism. Days before I was to visit the health ministry with the purpose of entering my name for a place as a psychiatrist in Madrid, I spoke to a good friend from my course. She had a crazy but exciting proposition for me: let my place go—I could come back and do the exam a year later—and go to Cambodia to work for an NGO that she and her family had collaborated with for a while. I was thrilled by the idea. Minutes before my number was called at the ministry, I got up and walked out. I called my parents who, gobsmacked, couldn't believe what I'd done. I spent the next few days planning my trip.

I didn't know much about the history or way of life of the Cambodians, so I went to a bookstore on Calle Serrano, in Madrid, that sells travel books, and I bought a few on Buddhist culture, the history of Cambodia, and the traditions of Southeast Asia. Suddenly my attention was caught by one book in particular: *The Road of Lost Innocence*, by Somaly Mam. Written on the back was a brief summary of her life: she had been sold to a Cambodian prostitution ring and had spent more than ten years working in brothels until she fell in love with a client and managed to leave.

She founded one of the main NGOs fighting against people-trafficking, sexual abuse, and prostitution. The book was dedicated to Queen Sofía of Spain: "To Queen Sofía, for your constant attention to others. You gave me the strength to carry on my struggle."

I bought the book, which uncovers a world without morality, full of violations and aggressions. Those pages are the hardest I've ever read. They gave rise in me to a strong desire to meet this survivor, this fighter. I saw, over the course of the book, that in some ways Somaly hadn't managed to overcome all of the traumas and wounds of her past. Whenever she rescued another girl, her way of expressing herself revealed a pain that had yet to heal.

I tried to locate her, searching on the web, looking at her foundation and so on. I wrote a few emails but I never got a response. I knew that she had been traveling through Europe and the United States, denouncing this blot on humanity. I decided to help her, for which I would need to meet her. I would use every means necessary to cross paths with her at some point. The first step was obvious: I had to fly to Cambodia.

The planned flight itinerary was Madrid-London-Bangkok-Phnom Penh. Arriving in London, a storm delayed our landing by two hours, meaning I missed my connection to Thailand. I spent the night in a hotel by the airport and, the next morning, booked myself on another flight with another airline. At the gate, they told me that my luggage had been lost in the airport. They asked whether I wanted to wait until it appeared, or put in a claim for it at my destination. I got on the plane—I had decided to go to Cambodia and losing some suitcases wasn't going to stop me.

I landed in Bangkok. After a six-hour wait, I was able to take a flight to Phnom Penh. Once I was there, I hurried to the baggage office to put in my lost luggage claim. Next to me, a Cambodian lady was putting in her own claim. I stared at her; she looked like Somaly—from the book!—but I wasn't familiar with Cambodian facial types, so I wasn't sure. Just in case, I got the book out and put it on the counter.

"You have my book," she said to me in English.

I couldn't believe it, but it was her! A shiver ran down my spine. What luck! I told her, in a hurried, nervous way—I hadn't slept and I was flooded with emotion—that I had come to Cambodia to look for her, and that I had an idea for how to help her in her work with young girls. She didn't believe me.[*] She looked

---

[*] Somaly is a woman who has been profiled and persecuted by different mobs and organizations. In the last few years, articles and interviews have been published that are critical of her life and work. In these pages I describe objectively what I experienced—working in her foundation, the therapies we cooperated on, and my personal relationship to her.

around her for her bodyguard. It was one of the most exciting moments of my life and it was slipping between my fingers.

"There's someone you love very much," I added.

"Who?" she asked

"Queen Sofía," I answered, and she looked at me carefully.

"Do you know her?"

"We all know her!"

Finally she gave me a warm smile and said, "Here's my number, give me a call tomorrow!"

After this providential encounter I got to know a true fighter, pouring herself into helping other women in her situation. Through her I gained entry into the world of prostitution and brothels, carrying out HIV and STI prevention, and therapy on girls and young women who had been raped and abused—I even met Queen Sofía and worked with her on a few occasions, as she was interested in collaborating with Somaly.

I entered into contact with a terrible world, full of pain and physical suffering, but above all psychological anguish. I attended to women with authentic trauma, and in exchange I received the satisfaction of being able to help, to be of use in the midst of this underworld, to lend a helping professional and personal hand to people who had nothing. An experience like that enriches the giver more than the receiver, because it creates gratitude and helps you to value what you have more, and not to ignore those who are suffering. And all of this from a casual encounter at the airport, putting in a claim for lost luggage . . . Was it fate? Thanks to that moment, my life changed. I'm so lucky I missed that flight—and lost my suitcase!

Ascending Reticular Activating System (ARAS)

Every second, our mind captures a few million bits of information, but it only pays attention to what interests us, or feeds into our hopes or dreams.

Since we are exposed to a bewildering multitude of stimuli, the ARAS is charged with filtering and prioritizing among all this information those things that are relevant to our goals, worries, or survival. If our brains assimilated and paid attention to every stimulus, we would be completely overwhelmed.

When a woman is pregnant and walks down the street, she may think, "Look how many babies there are in the neighborhood!" In reality, there isn't a fertility boom. What's happening is that her brain is more "sensitive" to this particular type of information. If something interests us, the brain does what it can to find it among all the inputs we receive. When we're looking for a flat to rent, suddenly our brains notice signs in every window. If we're interested in a certain model of car, soon we'll be bumping into it at every traffic light. A lot of those notices and cars have probably already been there for a while, but we didn't have the intention or capacity to see them. Our minds were on other necessities.

If you really long for something, you'll be able to manifest it.

This doesn't mean that simply by wanting something you can make it happen the next day. The key is to give the brain objectives and aims, so that it's open to them if they pass by. The problem is that many people don't know what they "long for"; they just let themselves be carried along. For the majority of people, the fact that nothing interesting happens to them in life has a very simple cause: they don't know what they want to happen.

Think, imagine, and dream on a big scale. Act on a small one.

Use your imagination in a healthy way. If you really want something— within reason—and you imagine it in detail, you can achieve it. Let your heart fly, make a plan of action, and execute it. The plan is fundamental: Without a plan and short-term goals, good things remain out of reach. In the words of Bernard Shaw, if you have built castles in the air, that is where they should be—now put the foundations under them. Use your imagination. Dream. In terms of neurobiology, very significant things happen in the brain when you imagine something in detail, with excitement. Your brain undergoes a change; you've induced an emotional state that is capable of modifying the normal proceedings of your neurons.

In this life, we attract what we think about.

Focus on what you really want, use your passion to get excited about a big project—or a small one! It should be whatever awakens the deepest aspects of your being; you'll begin to feel something happening inside you. You'll gain security, confidence, and joy, and, even more surprisingly, your brain will change. States of excitement maintained over the duration of several days activate a process of neurogenesis: stem cells gravitate to the hippocampus—the memory and learning zone—and transform into neurons. We know very few ways of producing new neuronal cells, but passion and enthusiasm are two of them!

Every human being, if he chooses to, can be the architect of his own brain. —Santiago Ramón y Cajal

Your mind and your body are transformed when they see that good things can happen. It's not a question of being obsessed with achieving a specific goal—life doesn't always take you where you want to go—but of attaining a mental state that will guide you toward your BPS, or your "best possible self."* Remember that dwelling on a goal can also have the opposite effect; that is to say, it can prevent you from seeing interesting alternatives that arise in your life because you're only focused on achieving something very specific. Sometimes you need to take distance, get a wider perspective, and maybe direct yourself toward a different goal. We're always getting "signals" from life—you can call them what you like—that direct us toward the right path, the one where we can develop into the best versions of ourselves.

---

* In Chapter 9, we'll look at the formula for BPS.

HOW TO GET THE MOST OUT OF YOUR ARAS

- Every morning, when you get up, whether in bed or when you're drinking your coffee, choose a goal for the day. It could be something insignificant (speaking to someone, having a particular conversation or making a call) or a more important challenge that you're excited about (something that puts your brain in its optimal emotional state).

- Imagine yourself achieving this goal, with excitement, calm, and confidence. Feel it, relish it, enjoy it to the full. Just for a few moments—be careful not to let your imagination run away with you and lose time idly daydreaming.

- Think of the first step toward your goal and make a simple plan.

Have courage! You're close to achieving your goal: you've activated your ARAS, so it will now be easier to accomplish.

It's fundamental to open your mind. If we don't activate our attention—and our ARAS—we won't see the possibilities that unfold before us. If, on the other hand, we maintain a receptive, optimistic, hopeful attitude, we'll be capable of understanding what happens to us and give meaning to our experiences.

We have a problem: In this world we don't pay attention to what happens to us anymore, nor are we surprised by anything. Today society needs to recover a more attentive, curious way of looking at reality; if you observe anything with attention, it soon becomes interesting. This requires stopping and being able to listen to the silence. Silence is not the absence of sound! It's the capacity to look inside calmly, cutting off the racket outside.

Walk down the street with a child, and you'll realize how much captures their attention. From my house to the nursery my younger son attends is a distance of a third of a mile. It takes almost half an hour to walk there with him, and less than five minutes to come back. The reason? There are multiple "distractions" to attract his attention along the way: police cars, garbage trucks, people on motorbikes, planes, colored lights, shop windows, loud music coming from cars, strangers going by whom he has to greet . . .

LEARNING TO LOOK AT REALITY AGAIN

> *Knowing how to look is knowing how to love.*
> —Enrique Rojas

Observe the reality that surrounds you, take delight in it—you'll find that there's always something to be drawn to. Looking attentively reinvests life with interest and fascination. We should learn to look at reality with new eyes, without harshness. What's missing that would allow us to do so? Care and amazement.

I sincerely recommend looking again at your job, your family, your children, your house—but this time with amazement! Maybe you'll be caught by some detail that you've gotten used to without realizing, or maybe you'll rediscover positive things that you've been ignoring. This is particularly important in relationships; look at your husband or wife as though it were the first time, take note of their face, their body language; deepen your awareness of their gaze, the way they relate to others and you. Don't ever get used to the person you fell in love with—it requires attention not to be ground down by routine.

If you look at reality with indifference or ennui, taking everything for granted, without stopping to take notice of subtleties, you'll likely get bogged down by the same things over and over, stuck in negativity, difficulty, and problems lacking simple solutions.

CASE STUDY: EMILIA

Emilia has been divorced for eight years. She had been with her husband Juan for twenty, and was very much in love with him. They had three adolescent children, aged 19, 17, and 16. Their relationship worked well and they respected and loved each other, experiencing ups and downs like all couples, but stable on the whole.

Juan began traveling to the United States frequently for his work. He spent long periods in New York, Miami, and Los Angeles. Emilia resented this—she was used to being part of a solid couple, and she noticed that relations between them were getting colder. And indeed, one day when Juan had returned from a trip, he sat Emilia down and told her that he had fallen in love with someone else. Emilia tried to dissuade him, to convince him otherwise, and took him to see various therapists, but he had made his decision. The other woman was young, only 27, and they were expecting a child together. Emilia realized that, even though she loved him, it would be impossible to forgive him.

The first four years were hell for her—she suffered, she cried all the time, and she fell into a severe depression. After receiving pharmaceutical treatment, she got better, and her medication was gradually withdrawn.

When she comes to see me, as I said, it has been eight years since the separation. She is accompanied by her eldest daughter, now 27 years old, a medical resident in a Madrid hospital. She tells me that her mother has never returned to her former self, and despite the passage of time, she has never recovered any passion for living. She explains that she has something negative to say about everything, she judges everyone harshly, and she looks at the world with scorn. She denies feeling sad or depressed and only speaks in order to criticize or judge others. She fixates on the tiniest details and finds something to be desired in everything around her. She's going to be a grandmother in a few months and her children are worried by her attitude.

When I speak to Emilia, I discover a woman who is "angry at life." From the first moment, she complains about the weather, the Madrid traffic, and how demanding her children are. During our hour-long interview, I can't get her to speak well of anything or anyone. I ask about her house at the beach—her daughter tells me that it's a very pleasant and charming place—and she remarks that it gets very dusty when it's shut up, and she doesn't enjoy going there in summer anymore.

When asked about her daughter, who's soon to be a mother, she tells me, "She'd better not be counting on me to help her when it's born, I already told her she was too young to be having children yet."

The daughter who has accompanied her confirms that she was truly depressed—she cried all the time and spent days in bed—but that now the dominant note in her personality is her constant complaining.

I explain to Emilia how important it is to look at her world again with fresh eyes. She looks at me, surprised. She asserts, with no hesitation, "I'm completely objective."

I emphasize that happiness depends on one's interpretation of reality. I map out her personality chart, taking into account happiness and beliefs, and explain that she has trapped herself in a role in which criticism and judgment reign over every impulse. She's incapable of visualizing good things, or looking at her surroundings with amazement, compassion, or tact.

We began a course of therapy that lasted ten months. I helped her to overcome the wounds of her past, not to hate the present so much, and to be capable of getting excited for the future. It wasn't easy, but today she's aware that her problem was rooted in how she was interpreting reality. Her attentive capacity, as she has said, "was infected."

An optimist looks you in the eyes and speaks from the heart; a pessimist looks at the floor, shrugs, and forgets to communicate with the heart.

Fix your attention. Try to concentrate.

José Ortega y Gasset, the great Spanish philosopher, was one of the most important thinkers of recent times. The author of "I Am Myself *and* My Circumstances" had serious concentration problems, due to the number of ideas crowded together in his head. To attain the mental state needed for him to be able to write, he required "self-absorption," which allowed him to abstract himself from the world outside. He would walk back and forth in the enormous empty hallway of his house, kept nearly dark. Once he was able to put his thoughts in order, he would sit at his desk to map out his ideas in a black spiderweb across the wall at eye height. This is how he maintained the inspiration that he found in his hallway.

What techniques do you employ when you really need to concentrate?

Look up, let go of your phone, see with new eyes and with your heart, and have hope that something will manage to astonish you!

In today's world, the Ascending Reticular Activating System (ARAS) is blocked. One of the main causes is the rise of the screen. It's very difficult to pay attention to the good things that arise in front of us. Having control over your attention is key. We must all learn to divert the stimuli that assault our sense without stopping, and to pay attention to what really matters.

NEUROPLASTICITY AND ATTENTION

Neuroplasticity is responsible for "rewiring" neuronal connections, from the establishment of new connections between cells to the adaptive phenomena that arise in the brain in response to changing circumstances and challenges.

Diverse factors, such as stress, illness, genes, infections, trauma, or accidents, can negatively influence this capacity. Activating your ARAS makes neurons connect, facilitating your ability, faced with a multitude of stimuli, to pick out what's important and necessary.

We sculpt the brain in real time, shaping it according to what we attend to and give our full attention.

In our brains, neurons work according to how we focus our attention. When you aren't capable of controlling where you direct your attention, when you can't concentrate adequately, the efficiency of your decision-making process is seriously affected. The good news is that we can "deconstruct" our disruptive mental automatisms, redirecting our attention to where we really want. Attention is an act of will, and therefore it can be trained.

> *To control our wills, we must be*
> *masters of our attention.*

Now begin to:

- Train your attention: try to focus on the positive things that surround you.
- Savor the present moment. I say "savor" because sometimes we get used to the information flowing in from our senses and stop paying attention to them. If you eat an orange, a banana, or a slice of ham, enjoy it. Really make yourself experience its scent, texture, and flavor. When you're next in a park, dare yourself to close your eyes and concentrate on your senses of hearing and smell. Don't let music just be a distraction—don't just hear it, *listen* to it.
- Decide. Take the reins of your life. Find something valuable, something objectively good in your environment, and take a minute to make positive remarks about it to yourself. You'll be surprised. Try to do this with people, events, circumstances, etc. There's a lot of good you're not noticing because you've blocked off this area of your mind. Don't forget that the mind and the body are one at the deepest level.
- Medication can help, but it's never the only solution to your problems. It may push you to get better, but you must work on your mind if you want to avoid falling back into the same position.

6

EMOTIONS AND THEIR IMPACT ON HEALTH

WHAT ARE EMOTIONS?

Emotions are affective states of greater or lesser intensity, the body's response to life's circumstances, everyday occurrences, and our subjectivity; they reveal our way of being, and they express the way we feel.

The same facts can elicit different emotions, and emotions are what give color and flavor to the events of our lives. But emotions are also related to physical and mental health. For example, if I say "I feel good," I experience well-being and peace; if I affirm that "I feel healthy," I improve my health; and if, conversely, I assert that "I feel alone," I experience loneliness.

POSITIVE PSYCHOLOGY

The term "positive psychology" was coined by American psychologist Martin Seligman in 1998. There are two ways of responding to events: with positive emotions or negative ones. According to which ones dominate and steer us, we'll feel one way or the other.

Let's look at this in more detail. The most studied emotions have historically always been the negative ones—pain, anguish, anxiety, rage, loneliness. Science has of late been investigating the positive emotions more, especially since the relatively recent appearance of positive psychology.

Another scientist of interest in this field is Richard J. Davidson, doctor of neuropsychology and founder/president of the Center for Healthy Minds at the University of Wisconsin–Madison. There, they investigate the positive emotions, behaviors, and qualities of human beings, such as friendliness, affection, compassion, and love. It all started after Davidson met the Dalai Lama in 1992, and he asked him this question:

"Has it never occurred to you in your work studying the mind to investigate friendliness, tenderness or compassion?"

Since then he has been researching positive emotions in human beings, guided by the motto that "kindness is the foundation of a healthy brain."

A STUDY WITH SURPRISING PARTICIPANTS

Doctors David Snowdon and Deborah D. Danner carried out a study on 180 Catholic nuns in the United States who had written short accounts of their lives at the average age of 22. These nuns were then analyzed 60 years later, on a number of dimensions. Researchers discovered a correlation between positive emotions displayed in their autobiographies and longevity: Ninety percent of those who had a quantifiably greater number of positive emotions were still alive at the age of 85, whereas this was only true of 34 percent of those who had demonstrated fewer positive emotions. In a later evaluation, 54 percent of those who displayed more positive emotions were still alive at the age of 94, while of the group with fewer positive emotions, only 11 percent survived. They also discovered that the nuns who expressed more thoughts or had richer vocabularies had a smaller chance of developing any type of senile dementia after 85, an age at which the risk of Alzheimer's is about 50 percent.

The study continued even after the death of its participants; the vast majority donated their brains for later analysis. At this stage, the chief discovery was that there was no clear relationship between pathology and symptoms; that is to say, nuns whose brains presented serious damage had demonstrated good physical and mental health, and the reverse was true too. Tissues were discovered to be intact in nuns who had shown clear symptoms of some type of senile dementia. They also discovered that the healthiest brains corresponded to the nuns who had lived for more than 100 years.

Oddly enough, Professor Snowdon began the study completely by chance. He visited the convent to investigate the dietary habits of the religious community, and their effect on aging. Once there, he realized that they formed an unexpectedly interesting study group, with ideal characteristics for research, such as low stress levels, and no alcohol or tobacco consumption. Seven of the nuns in that convent lived past 100: They were known as "the magnificent seven." The study received an official grant of several million dollars due to the interest it provoked.

This brings us to a very interesting conclusion: senility and mental aging do not appear to be inevitable, however ancient we are. The key seems to reside in positive emotions.

THE PRINCIPAL EMOTIONS

Many authors have gone into this question thoroughly, detailing the emotions and studying them in different countries and societies in order to come to a consensus. The American psychologist Paul Ekman—a consultant on the Pixar film *Inside Out*—has studied the emotions in depth, along with the ways we demonstrate what we're feeling through facial expressions or body language. Why do we shrug when we feel sad? Why do we gesticulate differently when experiencing disgust or fear?

Ekman created what is known as the Facial Action Codification System (FACS), a taxonomy that measures the movements of the 42 facial muscles, as well as those of the head and eyes. Through this system, he established in 1972 that there are six universal facial expressions, related to what he considered the six basic or primary emotions: anger, disgust, fear, happiness, sadness, and surprise.

THE MOLECULES OF EMOTION

Now we're getting into exciting territory. The American neuroscientist Dr. Candace B. Pert, who died in 2013, was director of NIMH, the National Institute of Mental Health, and author of the bestseller *Molecules of Emotion*, about the effects of emotion on health. She provoked a true revolution with her studies on the mind-body connection and was also the discoverer of the opioid receptor.

I'll try to give a simple explanation of her discovery. Opioid receptors can be found on the surfaces of our cellular membranes, and they bond selectively with specific molecules of the key-lock type. The molecules that reach the receptors are called neuropeptides. These form the basic substratum of emotion.

What's interesting is that each and every emotion activates the production of these neuropeptides. When a receptor in the membrane receives a molecule of emotion—a neuropeptide—it transmits a message to the interior of the cell. This message can modify cellular biochemistry and frequency, affecting its behavior.

What are we referring to when we talk about cellular behavior? Anything from the generation of new proteins or cellular division to the opening or closing of ionic channels or even the modification of epigenetic expression—genes! That is to say, these neuropeptides act as mechanisms that alter our physiology, behavior, and even our genes. Part of a cell's "history" derives from signals that the neuropeptides of emotion send through the membrane.

According to the words of Dr. Pert, "neurotransmitters called peptides carry emotional messages. As our feelings change, this mixture of peptides travels throughout your body and your brain. And they're literally changing the chemistry of every cell in your body."

Due to this and other discoveries, she is considered the founder of what is now called psychoneuroimmunology.

Illness is therefore unavoidably associated with the emotions. When an emotion is expressed, the body responds. When an emotion is negated or repressed, it remains trapped, seriously damaging the individual. As Dr. Pert says, every emotion has a biochemical reflection inside the body.

DROWNING IN SWALLOWED EMOTIONS

There's a saying in Spanish: if you keep swallowing, you'll drown. In the last few pages, we've discovered the importance of thoughts and emotions for our health and conduct. Let's look at a concrete example.

If someone says to me, "Your outfit is horrible," I can react in a variety of ways:

- Replying "You're horrible."
- Bottling up my emotions, becoming resentful and sad, and going over and over the incident: "Why did they say that to me? It's not that bad, is it? What do they have against me? Should I have dressed differently?"
- Blocking and denying what happened, not thinking about it, ignoring it.
- Replying along these lines: "Well, I like it, I've always had unique and original taste."

Each response has a different impact on the body, on each cell, and, of course, on the mind. In the first case—where I respond in an impulsive, direct, and even slightly aggressive way—perhaps my body isn't altered, but I'll end up losing friends and breaking or complicating many personal relationships. The second and third cases will make me ill. I'm silencing and blocking negative emotions, and this has repercussions on my physical and psychological health. Freud explained it in this way: "Repressed emotions never die. They're buried alive and will come to light in the worst way." The final response is the healthiest. But it's not always possible to act and respond in the best possible way. Sometimes our personalities or circumstances make us take unexpected or inadequate actions, and we only become aware of it sometime later.

We live in a society that incites us to block and deny our emotions. This is due to the fact that appearing to feel things or get emotional is a sign of weakness or a lack of strength. At times it even seems inadequate or inappropriate to express what one is feeling, especially if it has an emotional component.

Those of us dedicated to the world of the mind and emotions know that repressing an emotion is equivalent to refusing to accept it. These emotions remain sealed off and stored in the subconscious. It's only logical that they should crop up in one way or another at some point in our lives, profoundly disturbing our equilibrium. A clear example can be found in the instances of depression that occur during pregnancy or in the postpartum period, both moments of great vulnerability for women.

If one keeps one's feelings in check for fear of what others will think, afraid of looking ridiculous or incapable of expressing oneself, that will end up causing damage. Emotions build up and can harm us—like menacing shadows falling over our bodies and minds.

LEARNING TO EXPRESS YOUR EMOTIONS

When one isn't capable of emotional self-expression, sometimes one hopes that other people will realize when harm has been done. The reality is that, in the majority of cases, those who judge, criticize or wound us don't do so with ill intent. They may even be ignorant of the damage they're causing to others. There are people who enjoy offending and aggravating others, but they're a minority. In such cases we may even be dealing with people with severe personality disorders. Someone affected by an antisocial disorder, commonly called a psychopath, enjoys wounding others and does so with the intent to inflict harm.

On the other hand, there are people with heightened sensitivity and vulnerability to the comments and actions of others. They have excessively thin skin, psychologically speaking, and have to be treated with great care, because they feel offended at the slightest thing.

CASE STUDY: BEATRIZ AND LUIS

Beatriz and Luis have been married for six years. They have three small children—the oldest is three, and they have one-year-old twins. Luis is an architect who for many years worked and traveled a lot, but in the wake of the economic crisis he has suffered considerably; he's changed jobs and now he accepts freelance projects to supplement his finances. Luis is direct, impulsive, quick and efficient, and a perfectionist. He fixates on details and likes everything to be just so. He sees things with clarity and expresses what he's feeling at any given moment.

Beatriz is an interior decorator—they met on a project, remodeling a building of cultural significance in the north of Spain, and they quickly got together and married. She comes from a family where she is the oldest of four sisters. She has a very close relationship with her sisters and her mother. She's always been very sensitive. Her father was sick for many years with kidney problems, and she has always helped her mother with everything. She tends to swallow or bottle up everything bad that happens to her, so as not to worry anyone else.

Beatriz comes to see me because for a few months now she's been sad, apathetic, and lacking strength. She connects this to the birth of the twins, but it's already been a year and she isn't getting any better. She can't enjoy anything; sometimes during the day, when Luis is working, she locks herself in her room to cry, something she tries to hide from her children.

When her husband comes home, tired and irritable—it takes more effort to earn the same money now—he sees toys on the floor, a messy house, and the children crying, and he starts shouting, giving orders to tidy everything up quickly, for the children to eat dinner at once, and for them to be quiet so he can sit in the living room watching the news without anyone bothering him.

Beatriz, silenced, doesn't say anything, but tidies, cleans, prepares food, and when the children are in bed, she just wants to cry again. Luis doesn't realize—he's caught up in himself and his worries, and Beatriz doesn't say anything. Not a thing, because she doesn't know how to say it; she doesn't know how to express herself.

When Beatriz first comes to see me, she tells me that a few days earlier, she was diagnosed with irritable bowel syndrome.[*] I carry out a complete interview during which she tells me her family history. She recognizes that she has never known how to confront her husband, or anyone she's close to, and that she seeks to avoid conflict. She prefers maintaining surface harmony to answering back or saying that something doesn't seem right to her. Lately, apart from her digestive symptoms, she's been experiencing vertigo and nausea. Psychologically, she admits that she doesn't take pleasure in anything, and she has memory lapses and difficulty concentrating.

---

[*] Irritable bowel syndrome (IBS) is characterized by abdominal pain and changes to one's digestive rhythm. The exact cause isn't known, although we do know that it has a significant emotional-psychological component. The intestines are connected to the brain in various ways through neurological and hormonal processes. Faced with stress, worries, or sadness, these receptors become more sensitive, worsening the symptoms. The condition is more frequent among women. It's diagnosed when an individual has symptoms at least three days a month over three months or more. It consists of abdominal pain, feelings of inflammation and strain, bloating, and a change in digestive rhythm, whether to diarrhea or constipation.

When we have a session with her husband, Luis doesn't understand how she can have gotten into this predicament. He explains that his wife has a big heart and never gets angry. He recognizes that he has an explosive personality, but says his wife "deals with it very well." I explain to each of them separately, using a chart, how their minds, emotions, and behaviors function in response to external stimuli; Beatriz, in response to the shouting and impatience she experiences from him, and Luis, in response to financial and professional frustration. I put their two personality charts together so they can understand each other, and I give them some very concrete guidelines for improving their relationship.

After a few months of therapy, Beatriz is better. I prescribe an antidepressant medication to improve her mood, which helps her to regulate her physical symptoms. Luis is prescribed a mood stabilizer to short-circuit his impulsive moments. After undergoing psychotherapy, the relationship improves significantly. Each has a better understanding of how the other functions, but above all, they are learning to manage their emotions in a healthier way.

So, if we don't express how we feel, there's a strong chance that the person in front of us won't be conscious of the harm they're doing. Women, in general, are more sensitive than men, and because they dwell on things more, they suffer more. This is aggravated by the fact that in many cases male partners—due to a lack of time, attention, aptitude, or all of the above—don't know how to read the subtle external signs that women sometimes use to try and communicate. Men tend to be less emotive and more pragmatic. In today's culture, women have a greater capacity for teaching how to love, feel, and self-express than men do. Of course, as in all things, there are exceptions to the rule, but this is the most common dynamic I encounter in my practice.

I'm not saying that it's necessarily good to blurt out the first thing we feel or that comes into our heads, but neither is it healthy to omit any conversation with our companions about something that is hurting us. The important thing is to achieve equilibrium between situations in which it is necessary to express oneself emotionally, and others in which it is better to keep silent in order to safeguard our inner peace and external harmony.

WHAT HAPPENS TO REPRESSED EMOTIONS?

We've noted that repressed emotions will return through the back door at some point, in the form of physical or psychological illness. I would consider "neurotic" those people who, incapable of handling their emotions in a healthy way, get stuck in the past. They're ground down by events, thoughts, or feelings that haven't been overcome or have been badly processed, and this transforms their characters, turning them into unwell people, exhausting to relate to.

We've already seen how positive emotions facilitate longevity, prevent the appearance of illnesses, or contribute to their cure. Negative emotions, on the other hand, can favor the appearance of illness.

CASE STUDY: EMILIO

Emilio comes to see me one day to find out the diagnosis and recommended treatment for his 14-year-old daughter, who has been in therapy for a few months because of bullying, which had given rise to problems with her mood and changes in her behavior.

He avoids coming to sessions with his wife, because he doesn't consider his daughter's therapy necessary, and everything relating to psychology seems to him to be useless and absurd. He greets me coldly and sits down. In cases like this I try to discuss trivial matters until I see that the atmosphere has warmed up. A few minutes in, I start talking to him about his daughter and how much she admires and loves him. Suddenly, I notice that his voice is slightly broken, and he changes the subject.

"Is this making you emotional?" I ask him.

"I don't like to get emotional or to feel anything intensely. It's a sign of weakness, and sentimentalists don't get very far in life."

"Ah! Big mistake. Sentimentality and emotivity aren't the same thing."

After that day I begin a very interesting course of therapy with Emilio. We dive into his life story: he comes from a wealthy family, with an American father and a Spanish mother. His mother is cold, emotionless, and has never allowed expressions of affection in their family setting. He never saw a gesture of affection between his parents at home, not a hug, a caress, or even an "I love you."

When he was little he had a neighbor he talked to a lot, but he moved away, and Emilio never again confided in anyone completely. Interestingly, the day he speaks about this neighbor, whom he hasn't seen in thirty years, he gets very emotional and cries. I've already explained to him that my consulting room is an appropriate place to cry. Nobody is judging or criticizing him. Tears are a powerful source of liberation from anguish.

WHAT DOES CRYING DO?

Never forget that the only species that cries for emotional reasons are humans. When someone observes another person crying, prosocial emotions or behaviors are frequently triggered in the observer, moving them to empathize. It therefore makes sense to assume that at some point in the evolution of *Homo sapiens*, tears became a way of expressing the emotional state of an individual's mind.

The body produces more than 25 gallons of tears a year on average. If we think of all the people who can't remember the last time they cried, we must also remember others who compensate by crying gallons and gallons of tears!

There are three types of tears: basal tears (which serve to keep the eye hydrated), reflex tears (provoked by physical shocks, dust motes, fumes, etc.), and emotional tears.

Emotional crying is prompted when the body perceives a state of alert— sadness, anguish, danger—and sends tears to the eyes as a reaction. At the same time, an increase in heart rate and blushing may occur.

THE BENEFITS OF A GOOD CRY

In 2013, a therapy arose in Japan known as *rui-katsu*, which can be translated as "the search for tears." Japan, for various cultural and historical reasons, is one of the nations of the world most lacking in emotional education. It is not socially permissible to express emotions. This technique helps people to liberate tension and repressed emotion, and recover inner peace.

The technique is a group therapy based on crying. People are encouraged to avoid doing it alone because of its resemblance to a depressive state in which someone might seek to be alone in order to cry and let everything out. The first *rui-katsu* was organized by an old Japanese fisherman, Hiroki Terai, in 2013.

The process is as follows: in a room with 20 or 30 people, videos, announcements, or short films with an elevated emotional charge are projected, until the attendees begin to cry. A session lasts approximately 40 minutes. The result is that people go away flushed out, relieved, and with a genuine improvement in their mood.

The researcher William Fey carried out a study a few years ago of the biochemical makeup of tears gathered from intense weeping caused by anguish or extreme sadness. He found elevated levels of cortisol. This is why one feels liberated after a bout of crying: it discharges tension and uneasiness by shedding significant quantities of cortisol.

PRINCIPAL PSYCHOSOMATIC SYMPTOMS OF BLOCKING THE EMOTIONS

When emotions turn into physical illnesses, we are dealing with what is known as psychosomatic illness (*psyche*, "mind," and *soma*, "body"). A psychosomatic illness is an affliction that originates in the mind but whose effects are felt in the body.

When a person feels embarrassment or shame, their cheeks blush. It's an involuntary reaction and it can't be consciously modified. When two people argue, their blood pressure may rise. Faced with a presentation, an exam, or a speech, one might experience tachycardia and hyperhidrosis (excessive sweating).

A high percentage of people who suffer from chronic stress, anxiety, or depression suffer physical symptoms such as migraines, back pain, muscular stiffness, gastrointestinal disruption, or other manifestations such as vertigo, nausea, or tingling in the extremities. The problem arises when the illness that has installed itself in the body is more serious, from gastritis with associated ulcers that require surgical intervention, to incapacitating neurological or oncological illnesses.

The principal psychosomatic disorders are:

- Related to the nervous system: migraines, headaches, vertigo, nausea, tingling (paraesthesia), and muscular paralysis
- Related to the senses: double vision, transitory blindness, and aphonia
- Related to the cardiovascular system: tachycardia and palpitations
- Related to the respiratory system: tightness in the chest and shortness of breath
- Related to the gastrointestinal system: diarrhea, constipation, acid reflux, pharyngeal pouches, and difficulty swallowing.

Don't forget: Long before it fell ill, the body was sending us warning signals in the form of discomfort, weakness, or pain. The illness, in these cases, is a message sent by the body, which never stops communicating with us, hoping to achieve equilibrium and peace.

Living in an era of hurry and rush, where everything is developing at such an intense pace, we don't connect to ourselves internally, or we're unable to give voice to those symptoms that are warning us something isn't working.

Those indicators are fundamental if we are to avoid ulterior sickness, or at least to slow down the progress of our symptoms. The body has a double function: on the one hand, it listens to everything our mind says and, on the other, it speaks to us through pain, unwellness, psychological unease, or disorders.

It is often said that anxiety is a fever of the mind and soul, warning us that our environment is hostile or that we're submitting our body to an excess of activity, emotion, or a situation it can't withstand. These processes of discomfort or pain—everyone has their own!—are therefore asking us, shouting at us to take notice of what's harming us, what's presenting a threat, or something that is becoming too much for the body and the mind.

> *Ignoring the body's signals is the first step towards*
> *weakening our health and creating an imbalance.*

Some discomforts may be due to bad habits having to do with nutrition, poor sleep hygiene, a sedentary lifestyle, or bad physical posture. If we're capable of taking a good look at our lives, with honesty, and without searching for a perfection that creates more anguish than peace, we'll be on the right track. We have to allow ourselves a bit of time to analyze our lives and consider what we're achieving, our goals and objectives, all while observing and physically sensing our bodies, verifying if they're sending us signals, and deciphering what the causes might be. Sometimes the help of a professional—a doctor, or someone who understands the body and its connection to the mind—can be of material support.

Science shows us many clear examples of illnesses related to the emotions. Dermatologists have documented that certain skin diseases are prevalent among patients who experience resentment, frustration, anxiety, or guilt. Cardiologists have demonstrated that heart attacks are more common in aggressive, competitive people, or those who have developed chronopathy.* Gastroenterologists have observed a correlation between emotions like anxiety—over an exam or a job interview, for example—and intestinal or stomach ailments such as peptic ulcers. But, without a doubt,

---

* Explained more fully in Chapter 7.

it's in the field of oncology that the mind-body relationship is being investigated most thoroughly.

The American clinical psychologist Lawrence LeShan has analyzed the lives of more than 500 cancer patients and unveiled a significant relationship between depression and the appearance of cancer. Many of the people he studied had been flattened by the rupture of close relationships and had tried to repress their related emotions. These repressed emotions modified their neurohormonal equilibrium and were counterproductive for their immune response. I'll go into the oncological implications in more detail later on.

CASE STUDY: TOMÁS

Tomás, sixteen, comes to see me. He's the eldest of three brothers, a good student, and the child of an architect father and a housewife mother. For the past year and a half, he's been experiencing problems with his vision. It all started one day in class, when he realized that the blackboard looked fuzzy. He told the teacher, and that afternoon he went to urgent care with his mother. He was diagnosed with an accommodative spasm. They prescribed some eyedrops and sent him home. For a couple of days, things improved, but one day in the middle of class, he realized that he couldn't see anything at all. They visited another specialist to get a second opinion. He was assessed, and they carried out various tests, but the problem kept getting worse. His degree of myopia changed at every eye exam and the cause remained a mystery.

After visiting various specialists—among them some neurologists—he was scanned and given an MRI, but the results were completely normal, at which point he was sent to see a psychiatrist. When I see Tomás at my practice, I'm surprised at how calm he is despite the fact that he "can't see." We psychiatrists call this *la belle indifférence*. He says that he's gotten used to not being able to see and that it doesn't worry him. I interview the parents and discover in Tomás' personality very marked traits of perfectionism and rigidity. He demands a lot of himself, he doesn't allow himself to make mistakes, he's always skipping ahead of his class in school to do more advanced work and he always wants to know more—to "see" further than is necessary at his age and maturity level. His body is pulling him up short: He can't see anything at all. He was in therapy for a few months, and we worked on his way of perceiving himself and managing his emotions. Little by little he recovered his sight and hasn't had problems with it since.

There are many known cases of people who cease to speak, see, or even walk, all for emotional reasons. The body is wise. I remember, one of the first times I was on call, encountering a 38-year-old woman who had suddenly stopped walking at work. The traumatologists and neurologists had ruled out an organic pathology. The case was sent to the psychiatric ward and, after various therapy sessions of different kinds, she recovered mobility in her lower extremities. That was one of the triggers of my desire to deepen my understanding of the mind-body relationship.

ATTITUDE AS A KEY FACTOR IN HEALTH

Over the course of these pages I've talked about the importance of our thoughts to our state of mind, our interpretation of reality, and our health.

A healthy and constructive attitude may be the most powerful natural medicine available to us, as well as, perhaps, the least often remembered. In the six years of study required to earn a Spanish medical degree, barely more than one lecture is typically dedicated to this topic. Despite this, we doctors are very conscious of the importance of a patient's attitude to their prognostic. Clinical data show that positive feelings and the emotional support of family members, friends, and even the health professionals involved in treatment possess an unquestionable curative power. In addition, what a patient feels, perceives, or believes can be as relevant as their diet and lifestyle when it comes to facing, for example, coronary disease.

Americans Meyer Friedman and R. H. Rosenman carried out a study on 3,500 men over the course of ten years. First, they divided the subjects into two groups: the type A group comprised those individuals with more rigid, impatient, or chronopathic (time-conscious) characters; the type B group was more relaxed and tranquil. After this preliminary classification, they investigated the health of their subjects—asking whether they smoked, how much physical exercise they performed, measuring their blood cholesterol levels, and analyzing their diets. Subsequently, they waited to see how their subjects would get on. In ten years, more than 250 of the physically healthy subjects suffered a heart attack. It emerged that data about their diets and physical activity were unable to predict these results. The only datum capable of predicting what would happen, the only datum with diagnostic value, was the preliminary classification based on their mental disposition. The subjects classified as type A had an incidence of heart attacks three times higher than the type B subjects, independently of whether they smoked, had a healthy diet, or exercised sufficiently.

AND . . . WHAT ABOUT CANCER?

Cancer would appear to have some relationship to stress and the emotions. The process isn't clear, but more and more scientists are voicing their instinct that emotions or stress can be risk factors in the development of cancer. As you would expect, oncological diseases possess varied and complex etiologies. There are as yet no serious studies drawing a direct relationship between emotions and cancer, but we all know someone who has suffered enormously in life and one day tells us, distraught, that they've been diagnosed with a serious illness. In our heart of hearts we aren't surprised: "After all they've suffered!"

In a project directed by the epidemiologist David Batty and carried out jointly by University College London, the University of Edinburgh, and the University of Sydney, sixteen studies completed over the course of a decade were analyzed. A total of 163,363 people began the study, and of these, 4,353 died of cancer. They were looking for the relationship between certain types of cancer, hormonal components, and lifestyle. At this point in the book, you know that depression generates a hormonal imbalance with elevated cortisol levels. This halts necessary repairs to the DNA and inhibits the adequate functioning of the immune system. The study results showed that people with depression and anxiety had an 80 percent higher incidence of colon cancer and twice the incidence of pancreatic and esophageal cancer. One has to read these results with care and not be blinded by their force: don't forget that anxious and depressive people have higher levels of alcohol and tobacco consumption, and obesity—three of the most common and most studied factors in cancer.

Cancer is related to multiple causes—environment, nutrition, toxic habits, genes—but a theory being postulated more often and with ever greater conviction is that the emotions also play a role. For a tumor to develop, various factors must coexist.

Cortisol, which we've already discussed, is a hormone that, maintained over time at abnormally high levels, provokes inflammatory processes that are harmful to the cells of the body. In July 2017, Dr. Pere Gascón, who was until recently head of the Barcelona Hospital Clinic Services, acknowledged in an interview that "chronic emotional stress can initiate the development of cancer."

This oncologist is one of the most renowned researchers into the relationship between the mental-nervous system and cancer. I'll try to explain this theory in simple terms. To begin with, don't forget that all oncological illnesses possess extremely complex developmental processes. I want to avoid any kind of reductionism around this very serious topic, but I think that a simple sketch can help you to understand the issue and pick out the broad strokes of how the body reacts to certain stimuli and the related importance of our mental equilibrium.

As we know, cortisol generates inflammation by releasing substances like prostaglandins and cytokines and is activated by situations creating chronic stress. Then we have tumors, each of which is a conjunction of malignant cells that take root and grow in some part of the body. With cancer, once the tumor is installed somewhere, the immune system—the body's defenses—stop attacking the tumor and "join its team."

For example, macrophages—a subtype of white blood cells—are charged with eating up the body's extraneous material. They form part of the innate response of the body's defense system. In the case of cancer, they stop functioning and start "working for" the tumor. The body's own immune system shows an auto-aggression toward it.

In the body, there are between five billion and 200 trillion cells, depending on an individual's age, sex, and other characteristics. Around these cells is blood, whose composition is determined by the purpose of the cells. What controls the blood? We've looked at this in previous chapters: The neurohormonal system is key. Researchers have uncovered a curious fact: if they put a cell into a toxic environment, it gets sick. If I surround it with a healthy environment, it heals. The cellular environment, as much as the information received by its membrane, plays a fundamental role.

*Just as occurs on a cellular level, if a person—
a conjunction of cells, and of course, a little
something more!—it frequents a toxic environment,
whether the toxicity is due to people, atmosphere,
or adverse circumstances, they'll get sick.*

Careful! If, despite being in a healthy environment, the mind interprets it as threatening, it will go on the alert and provoke the same changes in the body and the composition of the blood as if it were in the most toxic possible atmosphere. Don't forget, the mind and the body don't distinguish reality from imagination. There are people who, despite being situated in a relatively normal environment and average circumstances, live constantly on the alert. These people, through insufficient focus on their actual situation, force their bodies, both physically and psychologically, into a harmful state of tension.

If I'm capable of changing the way in which I interpret reality, reality changes. Happiness depends on the interpretation of reality that I make! It's fundamental to accept a change in my beliefs, myself, or what surrounds me—without judging myself too harshly. From there, the benefits of fomenting positive thoughts, or even of deliberately calling on the placebo effect, can have an effect on my mind and body.

WHAT HAPPENS IN METASTASIS?

Now we're getting into an area of research that is currently developing very quickly. Metastasis, the process of dissemination of a tumor, which determines the prognostic and survival of the patient, often arises in a spot where an asymptomatic chronic inflammation already exists. That is to say, the cancer disseminates itself, develops, and progresses in inflamed nuclei. These form its microenvironment, the place where it feels most "at ease" and able to grow and expand. Not all inflammations carry the same risk of forming a breeding ground for cancer. Catarrh (inflammation of the amygdala) and strained ligaments (with muscular inflammation) aren't of this type. A smoker, every time he or she smokes, damages his or her bronchial cells, producing a chronic inflammation of the area. This inflammation arises in order to defend and safeguard the area; in principle, this is a good and healthy thing. But if the vice of smoking and consequent inflammation are maintained over time, and if, in addition, this person has a precedent for lung cancer in his family, and if, finally, we add to this explosive cocktail a serious emotional problem, this person is a likely candidate for cancer. Of course, not all smokers get cancer, but we know tobacco is a potent activator of oncological processes. This is why patients are asked how long it's been since they smoked at medical checkups—it's pertinent to know how much time the body has been granted to recuperate from the constant assault it was submitted to, accompanied by the whole inflammatory process occurring during a patient's years as a smoker.

Studies have proliferated in this area, with astonishing results. It's been discovered that there's a direct relationship between cancerous cells and the nervous system. That is to say, there are receptors on tumorous cells for substances related to the brain, such as adrenaline or cortisol. The emotions and the impact of severe stress alter the body, but they also affect cancer cells. Direct communication occurs between a cancer and the mind—it touches the nervous system, and therefore the emotional system as well.

The aim of this explanation is not to upset or disturb the reader. On the contrary, it should serve to help you understand even better the profound connection that exists between the most serious, difficult to control illnesses and our minds.

Cancer has deep links to the immune system. Stressful situations, worries, sadness, and chronic trauma alter our defenses and increase the likelihood of developing a serious illness. These emotional states are reflected on the physiological and biochemical levels, by latent inflammatory states.

To sum this up, harmful emotions in themselves do not produce cancer. That said, chronic emotional stress can trigger, activate, or accelerate the spread of cancer from its origin point. What provokes emotional stress? Situations like loneliness, having an ill family member, bad relationships with those around you, unresolved trauma, grief, or financial or work-related problems.

Being capable of positively redirecting our thoughts has a huge potential to help us control the level of inflammation in our bodies.

SIMPLE STEPS FOR MANAGING EMOTIONS WELL

1. Know yourself

Learn to understand what upsets you. If you have always blocked your emotions, it will be more difficult for you to explore the origins of certain problems. But try anyway—do some reading and speak to people who can help you. The first step is the most important.

2. **Identify your emotions**

   Put a name to what you're feeling. Rage isn't the same as resentment, nor is feeling joy the same as being moved. Be realistic when you do this, and don't blow harmful emotions out of proportion. This analysis has a direct impact on your body.

3. **Try to be assertive**

   Say what you think, without being hurtful. Don't silence your emotions, speak to someone you trust. Learn to express yourself, but be careful when you do—you might end up opening doors you can't close afterwards. Go little by little. Unburdening yourself should allow you to recover inner peace and equilibrium.

4. **Don't be afraid to become your Best Possible Self**

   Learn to give the best of yourself. He who denies his emotions ends up becoming a worse version of himself, a watered-down version without the capacity to feel excitement about anything.

5. **Place limits on the effect that others have on you**

   Learn to identify toxic people, who have the capacity to upset you deeply when you encounter them. It isn't possible for everyone in the world to disrupt your internal equilibrium, and you should try to keep your distance from those who do.

We all go through moments at which we experience displeasure or distress, when we feel anxious, apathetic, frustrated, or resentful. Experiencing negative emotions on occasion is a healthy thing: it alerts us to what isn't working in our environment and motivates us to roll up our sleeves and fix it, in order to restore our equilibrium both psychically and physically.

The problem arises when negative emotions become chronic, permanently modifying our state of mind.

Our way of thinking and feeling determines
the quality and duration of our lives.

TELOMERES

Telomeres, discovered by the American biologist and geneticist Hermann Joseph Muller in the 1930s, are the extremities of our chromosomes. Their principal function is to provide structural stability for the chromosomes, preventing them from getting tangled and stuck to one another; they're essential to cellular division. Because of all of this they're intimately related to cancer—don't forget that oncological illnesses presuppose an abnormal division of cells.

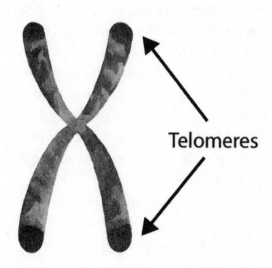

Telomeres are the timekeepers of our cells: They set the number of times that a cell can divide before dying and serve as the chronometer of cellular aging.

After earning her doctorate in molecular biology at the University of Cambridge in 1975, the Australian-born American biochemist Elizabeth Blackburn began studying chromosomal telomeres, first at Yale University and later at the University of California, Berkeley.

In 1984, while studying telomeres, Dr. Blackburn discovered a new enzyme, telomerase. She began creating artificial telomeres, with the aim of studying cellular division. She discovered that the lower the telomerase levels were, the smaller the telomeres were and, therefore, the fewer times a cell could divide, creating a greater risk of illness and aging.

Bad habits impact the longevity of a telomere—we're talking stress, diet, obesity, sedentary lifestyles, loneliness, pollution, or even sleep problems.

Blackburn studied telomerase in a specific group: mothers of children with severe neurological illnesses. She observed that those women who felt alone presented with lower levels of telomerase, with a consequent diminution in the telomere. Their life expectancy was much lower than normal for women of the same age. She also observed something fascinating: Those women who shared their feelings and supported and understood each other had higher telomerase levels and a consequent enlargement of their telomeres. For her work on telomerase, Blackburn received the 2009 Nobel Prize in Medicine, alongside her collaborators Dr. Carol W. Greider and Dr. Jack W. Szostak.

As we saw with Robert Waldinger's study,[*] loneliness is a risk factor for depression, but also for aging with shorter telomeres, making depression less healthy for us to endure.

How do we produce more telomerase and enlarge our telomeres? The first studies are now being carried out on how to foment telomerase secretion with the goal of achieving telomere enlargement. Positive effects have

---

[*] Chapter 2, on happiness and love for others.

been observed from exercising, eating a healthy diet, and practicing mindfulness. In 2017, in conjunction with one of the most important labs in the world, I began a study on the influence of mood and emotions on telomerase levels and telomere measurements. The objective is to confirm that cortisol, when chronically elevated, inhibits telomerase levels, and that anxiety shortens telomeres. I'm confident that interesting results will emerge, which will be published when the study concludes.

7

TRIGGERS AND ATTITUDES THAT INCREASE CORTISOL

There are a multitude of situations that can upset and harm us, altering our normal cortisol levels. We are immersed in a society that works, generates news and trends, travels, entertains itself, and even rests at a frenetic rhythm—sometimes we're unable to keep up the pace and we break down. There are certain emotional myths—being perfect, losing control—that have a more damaging effect on the body than we can imagine.

We mustn't forget that chronic stress is harmful and injurious to the body and the mind. On the other hand, eustress—good stress—is activated by the presence of a goal or a threat. This is what helps us to get going and look for the best solutions. We've all had moments when, under pressure, we've gone above and beyond. A classic example is the night before an exam. The brain suddenly memorizes more facts than it did during all the preceding days combined. Why? Small doses of cortisol improve concentration and the capacity to work efficiently, helping to focus the attention better in order to respond to challenges. But we can't always be under eustress; it will end up turning toxic, wearing us out, and making us ill.

Let's analyze a few situations that can result in a chronic rise in corti-sol levels.

CASE STUDY: ALBERTO

Alberto works as a communications director for a multinational company, and is transferring to their office in Mexico. Before going, he comes to see me because he's noticed that he's feeling sad, but doesn't understand why. Given that he's leaving in two days, I ask him to write to me from there, to see if it's a passing feel-ing or something more permanent.

Studying his case, I realize that he's a person who exerts excessive control over his life, over what he feels, what he expresses, or what he shows to others. His rela-tionship seems more like a job than a romance. Both members of the couple are executives, in both the professional and the emotional senses. They didn't want to have children, because they couldn't find the time for it, due to the demanding jobs they both have. Neither ever appears to have a low moment, and they always wear perfect smiles. Alberto maintains complete control over himself. Nothing changes him or gets him worked up. When I inquire about the cause of his sad-ness, he answers me, "There's no reason. Sadness is for the weak."

I add, "And is there anything that moves you?"

He responds, "Perhaps speaking to my father and spending time with him."

Alberto's responses are always too vague for me to probe with my questions. He tries to maintain absolute control over himself and over what he communi-cates to me. If he isn't very happy, he smiles. He's always very correct. Before say-ing goodbye to him in my office, I tell him, "If you carry on like this, you're going to break down. Any person who's constantly controlling themselves will end up crumbling at one point or another."

A few months later, I receive an email in which he tells me he's doing well and on his upcoming holiday he's thinking of returning to Spain. I indicate that if he wants to see me when he's in Spain he can, but he considers it unnecessary—he's currently stable.

One day in July, when I'm in my consulting room, the nurse alerts me that Alberto is on the phone and it's very urgent. I interrupt my session and go out to speak to him. On the other end of the line, Alberto, panting, nervous, and upset, tells me that something's happening to him. "We're in Málaga, in the middle of our holiday. This morning when I got into a taxi I started feeling bad, I couldn't breathe normally."

He needed to get out of the taxi at once, nauseated and experiencing vertigo, trembling, sweating, a sensation of losing control, and an intense anguish that wouldn't go away. He was having a panic attack.

His wife gets on the line because he can't speak, and asks me for help dealing with the situation. Despite her reluctance—she says it's only "something psychological"—I tell her to call an ambulance to take Alberto to Urgent Care as soon as possible.

Once at the hospital, his wife calls again. The medics have told him he needs to take a pill, and Alberto refuses. He, always so correct and balanced, has a terrible fear that the pill will make him lose control of himself, as much of his thoughts as of his behavior. I try to calm him down, explaining that he must accept the medication in order to *get* control and recover his equilibrium, but, beside himself, he roundly refuses.

His wife communicates a while later that the doctors at Urgent Care finished by injecting him with an anxiolytic to calm him down. Once he's discharged, they want to come to Madrid so he can begin comprehensive treatment.

A few days later, Alberto comes to see me in Madrid. He's anxious, alert, nervous, locked in an unending cycle of anguish, practically unable to walk down the street. I begin a course of pharmacological therapy with an intravenous medication—long-acting benzodiazepine—which blocks his fear and anguish circuits. I explain exactly what happened to him and the physiological and emotional mechanisms that brought him to this state. I prescribe an "emergency pill" to take if he has another panic attack, explaining that it acts within a few minutes. With this pill, he can travel and attend meetings, carrying "peace of mind in his pocket."

His greatest fear revolves around the idea that taking medication will make him lose the ability to manage life without it. To address this, every time he ingests a pill, I make him write in a notebook—and his wife also takes notes—sentences for him to repeat that neutralize this negative expectation: "Nothing's going to happen to me," "I'm not going to lose control or lose my identity," "I'm still going to be me," "These are the effects of the pill," "You can do this," "Don't give importance to sensations, don't overanalyze them," and so on.

After two weeks he's more stable, and we adjust the medication so he can take it orally. We also begin psychotherapy. Using his personality chart,[*] we explain his way of being and the apparent causes of his panic attack. I explain how cortisol and fear function, and we begin to explore some very exciting territory: the management of his emotions. If something seems funny to him, he can laugh; if something makes him sad, he can cry; if he's in an emotional situation, a reunion of family or friends, he can feel happy—nothing bad will happen.

One day during a session he confesses, "You're helping me to forge a vulnerable personality. Until now, I blocked my feelings in order to feel strong, but now I'm becoming capable of being moved, of feeling."

For him, so cold and cerebral, if someone lets themselves be carried away by their emotions, they become a slave to them, and suffering, pain, or passion can get in the way of correct decision making.

After a year of treatment, we begin withdrawing medication little by little; he has learned to navigate moments of high anxiety—he always carries his "emergency pill," which he's only used three times in a year—and, more important, he's turned into a warmer, more human, more affectionate person.

FEAR OF LOSING CONTROL

Human beings feel strong when they have control and are in the right. It is so hard to accept that we've made a mistake! The mind directs. The mind orders. The mind controls. We follow the directives of reason, responding

---

[*] See Chapter 4 for more on personality charts.

to questions exclusively from a cognitive perspective. In today's society, reason has become a tyrant, empowered by material and spiritual insecurity. The desire to control everything generates a huge amount of anguish. We think that having security in every aspect of life is a source of happiness. And indeed it's completely logical and prudent to procure the pillars of a secure, protected life: a stable job, a healthy family life, a comfortable financial situation. What's pathological, what's sick, is taking this to an extreme, distressing ourselves and embittering our lives in pursuit of an absolute security that can never be attained. Constantly looking for supports and material benefits that reinforce our lives and can't ever evaporate or fail us is utopian. That is where the error lies.

It's typical of our rational materialist society to make us believe that we can control everything: the point at which we get pregnant, the sex of our children or their academic brilliance, the type of work we do, our household income and spending, the perfect holiday, our health or the health of our loved ones, the perfect party. However, life teaches us that it can be difficult to get pregnant, and these difficulties are getting more and more common. Sometimes it's not possible to have one boy and one girl, or our offspring don't have the intellectual abilities we would have liked—although maybe they have other virtues that we, obsessed with intelligence, can't perceive in them. The business we've devoted our lives to can force us into early retirement. Income and spending are more and more uneven all the time. Maybe during a ski trip, a snowstorm shuts down the roads or the airport, or it rains on Paradise Island even though it isn't monsoon season. Even though we exercise every day, eat well, and get frequent medical check-ups, something can go wrong. Or when the day we scheduled our perfect party arrives, we find we're tired, sad, or overwhelmed and prefer to go hiking alone in the mountains.

Life is rich because of its variety, because it can't be controlled, and will resist any attempt to get an iron grip on it, however calculating one is, creating great anguish in whoever tries to control it. The Roman slave's whisper at the scene of a triumph is still relevant: *memento mori,* "remember that you must die." We mustn't lose sight of our own insignificance, we must be flexible, and practice the healthy art of letting go, enjoying the here and now.

> *The constant search for control prevents us*
> *from enjoying good things that are happening*
> *to us now, and makes us forget the present*
> *moment in our obsession with the future.*

If this control is rooted in dominating my emotions, my moods, and what I communicate to others, this has a malignant effect—as we saw in Chapter 6, you can drown in swallowed emotion.

CASE STUDY: ANTONIO

Antonio is the vice president of a company. The past weeks have been very tense, professionally, because the company is in the middle of negotiations to merge with a foreign multinational. One day, the president calls him to a special board meeting to discuss an important issue. Antonio is a very hard-working man, meticulous, extremely organized and consistent. He's shy, and for him, interacting with people requires an effort; he has to work hard to come out of himself, and only feels socially at ease when he's in situations where he's very confident.

When he arrives at the meeting, he finds thirty or so people around the table. The president takes the floor and says, "A few days ago I found out I have cancer; it's serious, but I'm going to fight it. I need to consecrate all my time and energy to getting better. Therefore, during my absence, I'd like our vice president Antonio to direct and coordinate the merger."

Antonio stands to say a few words, but he can't speak; he's suffering "aphonia." But a few minutes ago he spoke to his wife on the phone! He explains in a whisper, giving the first excuse that occurs to him, that he's recovering from bronchitis. He adds that he wishes the president all the best during his treatment, and that he'll lead the company as best he can during his absence.

He leaves the meeting and calls his wife; his voice is still faint, and he decides to see a throat specialist he knows at once. A few minutes into explaining to the doctor what happened, his normal voice returns. He doesn't understand at all. A few days pass and in his first meeting with high-ranking executives, when he's about to take the floor, the same thing happens! He can't speak. When he comes to see me he's afraid of two things: first, of speaking in public, a fear he already suffered from; but now he's also afraid of being "mute" in front of a group of people.

We begin the therapy with an explanation of exactly how to relax just before he's going to speak, using breathing techniques and repeating a series of messages that neutralize his fear. In a notebook, I draw a map for him, showing the nerves that touch the vocal chords, so that he can visualize the physical process and feel reassured on that count. In addition, we use sociotherapeutic techniques to overcome his fears and shyness in front of people.

During the president's cancer treatment, Antonio was able to direct the merger with success, and with a much greater control of people and of voice than he enjoyed before. All of this allows him to feel much more security in himself.

Exposure Therapy to Deal With Fear

This type of therapy consists of forcing the patient to confront the problem that causes his or her distress or irrational fear. It must be carried out little by little, to allow the brain to adapt and to allow the patient to feel secure with each step he or she takes.

In Antonio's case, exposure therapy consisted of first having him speak to the whole team at my office alongside his wife and another person he invited. Here, he gave a presentation on the structure and business of the company he worked for. Later on, we pushed him to say a few heartfelt words about different events he's attended—his son's first communion, or his cousin's wedding.

For people who suffer from agoraphobia, we usually recommend that a close friend or family member—someone they trust—accompany the patient to an open space. This is repeated at the next step, and the patient is left alone somewhere nearby, with an agreement to meet in another location. To all of this is added a series of useful breathing techniques, and internal affirmations of support for what the patient is doing. Little by little, the brain changes and adapts, and the body stops sending signals that it is anguished and overwhelmed.

How to Breathe

When someone says to a nervous person, intending to help, "Just breathe!", they usually think, "But I am breathing..." Obviously, when we ask someone to breathe when they're experiencing a moment of distress or anxiety, we're asking for deeper and more conscious breathing. Let's analyze this.

For a while now there's been a lot of talk about relaxation techniques, and there are multiple studies and articles on the topic. The majority of people believe that mindful breathing simply means inhaling deeply and exhaling slowly. They're not wrong, but here we're going to try to apply the idea in a more efficacious and organized way.

The first step is to find a comfortable spot that isn't too noisy. You could also dim the lights—switch off lamps, lower blinds, draw curtains—and put on some relaxing music.

Let's begin:

- Sit down on a chair—it should have a straight back but still be comfortable.
- Start by paying attention to your physical sensations. Focus on the feet. For the first few seconds, concentrate on feeling the weight of your entire body. Feel your lower extremities anchored to the floor. From there, move upward through the legs, the shoulders, the arms. Allow peace to suffuse your body as you enjoy the moment.
- Observe your breath. Before trying to "control" or "exercise" it, pay attention to the smooth movement of your abdomen as you inhale and exhale. Then turn your attention to the area around your nose as air enters and exits your nasal passages.

- After these first moments of observation and calm, we're going to begin with what's called diaphragmatic or belly breathing. This is more efficacious because it fills the area underneath your lungs with air, allowing for better oxygen absorption.
- Place a hand on your chest and another on your stomach, and observe which hand is lifted during inhalation. If the stomach lifts, you're doing it correctly.
- Draw air in deeply through the nose, hold it for a few seconds, and release it with control through the mouth.

One of the best-known breathing methods was designed by Dr. Andrew Weil, director of integrative medicine at the University of Arizona. He's been featured in *Time* magazine twice, and was interviewed by Oprah Winfrey about his theory of breathing. He recommends a 3-3-6 or 4-7-8 breath, depending on the number of seconds that the breath takes at each stage. In the case of 4-7-8, the breath follows this pattern:

- Inhalation lasts 4 seconds
- A pause, holding the breath, lasts 7 seconds
- Exhalation lasts 8 seconds

Practicing this technique at night while lying in bed can be very useful when trying to fall asleep. As with everything, it's good to start small, trying it out a couple of times per day, then increasing gradually. In this way, the body, the breath, and the sympathetic and parasympathetic nervous systems will learn to self-regulate.

When you're blocked or afraid of losing control, when stress is taking over, your mind is overwhelmed, or your body is failing to respond—breathe, take heart, and send yourself messages of peace and growth. This will get you out of the cycle.

PERFECTIONISM

CASE STUDY: LOLA

Lola is from Salamanca, married with two children, a five-year-old boy and a seven-year-old girl. She works as a clerk for the council, but she studied education and has always wanted to be a university professor. When she comes in for counseling, she's been working on her doctoral thesis for three years. She confesses that it's nearly finished, but every time she revises it, she finds things to tweak.

She tells me that she can't manage to relax at home—when she gets back from work she always finds the house is dirty. The people she hires to clean and help her with the children never last more than two or three weeks. According to her, this is because they don't do a good enough job. At work she's very demanding and never submits what's been asked of her on time.

In counseling, she complains about high anxiety and stress, and repeats several times that she "just can't anymore." Lately she's been unable to sleep and has been feeling irritable. At the next session, her husband accompanies her and remarks that for him, the issue of hired help is exhausting and always ends up monopolizing their conversations as a family.

"My wife is obsessed with cleanliness," he says.

He explains how, when she arrives home, she starts going over everything, running her finger along the furniture looking for dust, checking that the ironing hasn't been wrinkled, and that the clothes have been put away by color in the specific way she prefers. Nothing ever satisfies her, which invariably creates tension in the house, the marriage, and the family.

As a psychiatrist, I begin to wonder whether this person might have more than simple anxiety, perhaps suffering from some type of obsessive disorder. When I question her along these lines, she tells me that she washes her hands up to twenty times a day—when she touches food, when she pays with cash, etc.—either with water and soap when she's at home, or with antiseptic wipes when she's out. She's unable to go to bed with her husband if he doesn't smell the way she judges he should—she demands that he shower beforehand every time and that he use a particular brand of deodorant. When she furnished her house, she requested that the carpenter build cupboards according to the exact dimensions of the things they were going to contain, and the chests of drawers where she keeps her clothes were made to measure. She confirms that her mother and grandmother were the same. I ask her, "How much time do you take in the shower?"

She responds, "Oh, forty-five minutes or so."

She—on her own—goes through two or three big bottles of shower gel per week, because she needs to feel clean. I explain that she's suffering from an obsessive compulsive disorder that is provoking terrible perfectionism.

Perfectionists are eternally unsatisfied, in a state of permanent suffering because nothing ever meets their expectations. This type of person is great at finding flaws: They notice if something isn't clean or orderly; if it isn't harmonized; if there are streaks on the wall, a glass, or a mirror. Lola is very meticulous in her work, and when she's asked to write a report on something, she'll be double-checking it and verifying all is correct up to the very last minute. The same thing has happened with her thesis—whenever she rereads it, she finds errors to correct, and she never manages to finish it. She is a born sufferer, and the people around her are always on the alert, because she's always analyzing their defects.

One common trait of perfectionists is their rigidity when it comes to changing from one thought to another: They think about one thing and aren't capable of putting it out of their minds, creating a closed thought loop from which it's difficult to escape. In Lola's case, we prescribe a medication that works very well for this kind of disorder. In addition, we begin psychotherapeutic work with a notebook in which we mark down goals: these have to do with anything from cleaning, organizing, and the way she treats her husband and children to the recurrent thoughts that block her.

I emphasize learning to navigate moments of tension, with cognitive messages she can repeat to herself at those times when she feels the need to undertake her cleaning rituals: "Nothing's going to happen, you're fine, you're clean, remember that you have a disorder that prompts you to wash your hands a lot, because if not you can't calm down. Nothing bad is going to happen if you don't wash your hands this instant." Behaviorally, I recommend that she play in the park with her children without needing to clean herself before she gets home. Little by little, working on thoughts and behavior, she has substantially improved.

The Cingulate System

There is a specific brain area responsible for obsessions, compulsions, and mental rigidity. This is the cingulate cortex. Dr. Daniel Amen compares this area of the brain to the gearbox in an old car. The correct functioning of this area of the brain involves being able to change gear—or idea, or focus—easily. When we get stuck in one gear—or on one idea—the car doesn't function well, and, mentally, this produces what we call an obsession.

This is the area charged with visualizing different possibilities and options for any given problem, giving us greater or lesser flexibility in navigating the setbacks and changes of daily life. When it's working badly, or is over-activated, rigidity increases, and the probability of having toxic thoughts or getting stuck in a loop goes up.

A typical example of cognitive rigidity is the constant need to have things done when and how we want them done. There are people who have very marked obsessive traits, who are habituated to particular routines—almost rituals—so that any breach provokes a disproportionate reaction in them. Excessively rigid people need plans, schedules, and even the arrangement of rooms to be according to their hopes or desires. Perfectionists add another dimension: it all needs to be done in the best possible way.

Another Subtype of Rigid Person: The "Negaholic"

"No, no, no; I said no and that means no." We've all spoken to a telephone operator or a bureaucrat who ignores what you're asking for and gives an automatic, unjustified refusal. We have people in our lives who can't agree with us on anything. We deal with people who won't accept any advice or recommendations, and who never want to change.

For Dr. Chérie Carter-Scott, an expert on this type, "negaholics are those people who present an addiction to the negative." Whatever the situation, they constantly manifest a visceral, automatic, irrational negativity and are incapable of perceiving the positive or even the merely neutral. Their vision of reality is tipped toward the negative. Complaints and laments are the most frequent elements of their conversation.

This accumulation of negative attitude and commentary in the end does serious harm to the affected person. So-called negaholics are incapable of moving forward, and end up giving up on their own dreams, due to their unfounded fears and the pessimism that pervades their minds. They live in a state of constant anguish and suffering. Everything gives rise to toxic thoughts, which devolve into destructive speech and behavior.

This attitude alters their relations to others; it costs them a huge effort to celebrate others' successes, and they're always looking to "bring people down" with negative comments, expressions, and behaviors. Interacting with these people isn't easy, and those around them tend to want to keep their distance. They end up becoming obstacles for others, toxifying the environments they frequent.

Negaholics have many origins. Sometimes they're embittered by a personal trial they haven't overcome, other times after a traumatic period. After experiencing this pain, these people grow bitter and twisted; they break down or get depressed. The key, if you think you might be a negaholic, is to go outside yourself, ask for help as soon as possible, and recognize that this toxic internal process is seriously harming your life. A curious fact, according to studies carried out by Harvard University, is that 75 percent of people who have suffered a personal catastrophe have recovered after two years. At the very least, science urges us to be optimists in spite of catastrophe.

CHRONOPATHY: OBSESSION WITH
THE EFFICIENT USE OF TIME

THE ART OF RELAXING IS PART OF THE ART OF WORKING

John Steinbeck

We find ourselves living in a historical moment when the highest human aspirations are productivity and efficiency. This is what we call the commodification of time.

Today, everything related to velocity or the capacity to take better advantage of time is given a positive value. What is the consequence of this? The appearance of a particular stress, which, like a malignant disease, is extending into all aspects of our society, becoming chronic and seriously harmful.

Time is the most democratic resource there is. Every person in the world has 24 hours in their day. Everyone is responsible, not just for how they fill the day, but for how they perceive the sensation of time. Human beings define themselves according to the way in which they organize their days and, by extension, their lives. Organized people arrange it so that the hours multiply—don't forget that "order is reason's pleasure." At this point, we can differentiate between two extremes: those people who lose or waste their time, resulting in empty lives that lead to depressive states; and those people who suffer from chronopathy, or excessive time consciousness. We all know someone who's incapable of giving up any plans, who needs to arrange everything way in advance, and who fills every gap and opening in their diary with multiple activities. Be careful of these people—their lives end up turning into a desperate flight into the future. Don't forget that life's great experiences can't be savored amidst bustle, hurry, or while checking one's watch. Life is neither full nor gratifying without containing some moments of peace and quiet.

Do You Know How to Rest for Real?

I truly believe that rest—*real* rest—is in danger of extinction. A new syndrome has arisen: chronopathy—from *cronos*, "time," and *pathos*, "sickness"—the disease of time. As Gregorio Marañón said, "Speed, which is a virtue, engenders a vice, haste." We live with the conviction that hurry and acceleration produce more and better results in life. We're accustomed to hearing, if we try to set a date to meet someone, the response, "I don't have time, I'm too busy . . ."

We take this in stride, perceiving it as normal and correct.

Immediacy has become a key protagonist in our lives. We want everything, here and now. We can't wait a week to watch the next episode in a series, and we expect prompt refunds when our new kitchen tongs aren't delivered in 48 hours as promised.

Who hasn't experienced the sadness of a Sunday afternoon? I call it "gloomy Sunday." It's also known as "Sunday blues" or even "Sunday scaries." It particularly afflicts those whose lives during the week are especially intense. On Friday and Saturday, they rush around between different planned activities, most of which usually involve drinking alcohol. Sunday arrives, and they notice a dip in body and mood, which makes them wish it were Monday. The reason? They're racehorses who, week after week, arrive at the finish line with depleted resources. They don't know how to be in a state of rest. Any hiatus causes anxiety, feelings of guilt, emptiness, and sadness.

People today seem to need to use "a meeting" as an excuse to make themselves a space for leisure or tranquility. It doesn't look good to say that you're free or you aren't busy. How does this constant business and lack of downtime affect us? Suddenly, a friend calls, and very serious, with a worried gaze, reports that after suffering muscular problems, migraines, tachycardia, anxiety attacks, or even a heart attack, "My doctor has prescribed rest."

Then one begins to rebuild one's life, and a new phase begins, in which the meaningful things in life are given the importance they deserve.

CASE STUDY: FRANCISCO

Francisco is an executive in a multinational company who, when he was very young, sat the exam to be a government lawyer and got excellent results. Since then he's been on a meteoric rise: He began in public administration, and then he transferred into the business world. At certain periods in his life, he's been involved in politics, but without dedicating himself to it completely. In general, he's a man who loves to be taken up with as many matters as possible: politics, history, philosophy, and, naturally, law. He also likes to write. Because of this, his schedule is completely full from the moment he gets up until he goes to bed.

When he has free time, he gets overwhelmed; he likes the feeling that he's making the most of the time he has. When he's eating breakfast with his family, he asks everyone what their plan is for the day. He always finds a gap during which he thinks one or the other of them could take better advantage of their time if they did something different. His children spend their afternoons at school, attending extracurricular classes and activities—music, Chinese, English, art, sport—except for Friday afternoons, which he likes them to spend tidying their rooms and playing. On the weekend, he always has a perfect plan organized—going to the beach or the mountains, visiting another city. His wife lives "in his wake," and often tells him that she can't keep up the pace, that he needs to slow down, at which point he answers that we have to take advantage of life and seize opportunities as they pass.

He's begun to worry because he's starting to sleep badly and to suffer from migraines and occasionally from vertigo. He decides to see the doctor—after some difficulty rearranging his schedule, given that he has so little time—and he's prescribed some pills that have a slight effect. He's always living with a sense of being pressed for time and can't enjoy anything.

His family comes to see me with a specific request: "He needs to stop and learn how to do nothing."

But he insists that he doesn't want to stop, that this is his way of being, that if he slows down, it stresses him out, and he doesn't know how to live with calm.

I prescribe a medication for his anxiety in a very small dose—smaller than a therapeutic dose; the next day he calls to tell me that he's finding himself falling asleep at work. As soon as he slowed down a little bit, his body reacted as though he had ingested a brutal quantity of sedatives.

What we try to show him is that he doesn't know how to live in a state of relaxation. He himself recognizes that as soon as he detects a feeling of quiet or stillness, his anxiety wells up, and then sinks away again when he starts doing an activity. The most important thing for Francisco is not to teach him to relax—he's incapable of practicing relaxation techniques, yoga, or mindfulness, because they give him tachycardia—but to make him aware that he needs to learn to rest.

Becoming conscious of this—what we call insight—is his first step in therapy. The second is that he learns to do something that isn't wholly dynamic, that is to say, that he learns to "waste" time and relax. He achieves this with great difficulty, due to his strong internal resistance: he's always been this way, and his education and upbringing placed great emphasis on making the most of his time. His prognostic is therefore uncertain.

He's been in therapy for a few months, improving little by little. He's managed to grant his family spontaneous moments in which they're able to enjoy doing nothing or very little, or even improvising—something previously unimaginable.

Let's learn to stop. To slow down, in order to see, observe, and enjoy. Have you noticed that in order to really observe and contemplate something, you have to stop? When you're running you don't notice the beauty around you. Take delight in a beautiful landscape, a sunset, a captivating read; stop to enjoy wandering through a town hidden just off the beaten track, listen to a song that moves you . . . and do all these things without feeling guilty or like you're wasting time. This has benefits for our health, our enjoyment, our happiness, and our quality of life.

Jacques Leclercq explained this in his speech on joining the Free Academy of Belgium in 1936: the great philosopher René Descartes had visions and dreams over the course of several months of rest; Newton discovered one of the main principles of physics sitting under a tree; Plato constructed the pillars of philosophy in the gardens of Akademos. None of them arrived at their insights at a frenetic moment in their lives. It's not by running around in a huge hurry that we arrive at the deepest knowledge and experience of life's beauty.

Solitude, rest, silence, going slowly—all of these are keys to creating and beginning projects with excitement. The world is sick, effectively suffering from chronic stress. How will society function if we only produce hyperstressed beings, always running and operating at terminal velocity? A frenetic life indicates that our environment is directing us, rather than the other way around.

Listening to your inner voice is one of the first steps to understanding and overcoming yourself. This voice can't be heard over the frenetic clamor of daily life. Inner peace and ease are what all current therapies are asking for. In many places, every day sees a new yoga, mindfulness, or meditation class pop up, trying to disconnect from the external uproar.

We look at the clock so often that we don't give any time to what's important! Take advantage of a Sunday afternoon to disconnect from your phone and your watch; use airplane mode when you're at home, without worrying about missing a call, an email, a news alert, or a tweet. You don't need to be online 24 hours a day. Learn to "waste" a little of your time, thereby gaining in peace and serenity.

Don't take on too much. Learn to say no. Live in the present moment. Try to relish nature, the beach, the ocean, and the mountains, from time to time. You'll open yourself up to great experiences that will truly fill you up. Sure, do this without losing sight of your personal projects. Make plans, have checkpoints, but enjoy yourself whenever a special moment arrives, something you were hoping for or something that moves you.

THE DIGITAL ERA

I was coming back from Mexico, and imagine my surprise when I read this news in the paper: "Facebook admits to playing with the minds of its millions of users." This took place at a medical event in Philadelphia where Facebook's cofounder, Sean Parker, recognized that the business had been created to exploit "a vulnerability in human psychology . . . a social-validation feedback loop." The idea they proposed when they began the social network was to make users spend as many hours as possible there. That's how they had the idea of adding a "like" button to the platform.

What Happens in the Brain Every Time We See a Like?

Let's try to understand this mental and digital process. Those of us who are immersed in the study of emotions and behavior know that the universe of screens—internet, social networks, videos, and apps—is having a profound effect on the way we relate to each other, the way we process information—memory, concentration, multitasking, education, motivation—and therefore, in the long run, our happiness.

Nowadays, there are many businesses and programmers focused on making sure that individuals dedicate the greatest number of hours possible to their devices. This focus is conscious. That is to say, the makers of these devices know exactly how the mind functions in front of a screen or other technology, and they make apps to generate an addictive effect.

Essentially, recently developed gadgets and apps are designed to be addictive. This is something crucial and important to understand—as much for oneself as for parents and educators. Allow me to explain how this works.

Every addiction has a molecular and physiological base, something we've known for many years. Drugs like alcohol, cocaine, pills, or marijuana, or activities like gambling and watching pornography are all regulated by the same hormone: dopamine.

Dopamine is the pleasure hormone. It regulates the brain's reward system. It operates in the moment that an individual interacts with a pleasure object (sex, alcohol, drugs, or a social network) and in the moments leading up to that one—quite often merely anticipating pleasure activates the impulse. At times, it generates a posterior void, provoking a need to consume the product again within a short period of time. A person addicted to cocaine, sex, or social media experiences a profound impairment of their attentive capacity, has a modified will (regulated by self-control), and, in the end, comes to experience feelings of sadness and profound emptiness.

What did the cofounder of Facebook reveal at the event in Philadelphia? That every time someone gets a like, they receive "a little dopamine hit," motivating them to upload more content.

What's happening? Companies today aren't just carrying out traditional, conservative marketing; they're trying to bring together psychology, neurophysiology, and neuroscience. Hooking your mind and capturing your attention, they generate more content, more data, and a greater ability to control what you buy, what you see, what you decide, and what you do.

This is the foundation that drugs work from: mechanisms are activated in the brain, propelling us toward further, prolonged consumption of these substances. The majority of these products are either prohibited or regulated. We don't seem fully aware that children, from an early age, are exposed to this digital world—without any restriction—and with a huge possibility of profoundly altering their minds, their information processing systems, and their capacity to manage frustration and the emotions.

Every human being, beginning in childhood and adolescence, is looking for escape routes to navigate their highs and lows, their frustrations and their voids. Don't forget that screens have relaxing and learning functions as well. When children and young people find themselves in conflict, bored or stressed, they look to a device for relaxation. Their minds are accustomed, when faced with effort, to find a way out through the screen, social media, or the internet. A high percentage of the population flocks to platforms like WhatsApp, Instagram, Facebook, Twitter, and Tinder in search of that hit of dopamine that is triggered on contact. We're in the era of excess information and superabundant stimulation. This hyperstimulation has deep links to the immoderate consumption of information, as much as material or even fictitious goods. Everything is easily achieved, with just one click. When we don't get what we want when we want it, frustration circuits are activated in our brains, which are the starting point for the weakness of character of many young people, who are often lacking the ability to make any kind of effort—it's so difficult to wait for gratification! From this point arise numerous problems in education as well as some psychological disorders. I'm surprised—and very worried—by the number of young people I see in counseling who are suffering from extreme apathy and disillusionment; there doesn't seem to be a way of activating their attention and motivation. Don't forget that the only two things that really fulfill a human being completely are love (romantic or platonic) and professional satisfaction. These two pillars of life are achieved through effort, constancy, and patience.

Technological advances are progressing at an impressive speed, and preventing society from slowing down, stopping, and reflecting on the impact all of this is having on minds, bodies, and lives. When we're already completely saturated and, to some degree, altered, we raise our heads and look around us, trying to get perspective. In these moments—when voices are being raised on all sides—we ask ourselves: Is it too late? Have we created a monster that we can't control? The programmers of Silicon Valley send their children to schools where they barely even have computers. What are we losing?

Technology has brought us enormous benefits. Like anything, we have to relearn how to use it; each one of us needs to decide how we wish to direct our attention, beginning by looking at how we dedicate our time and later carrying out a real examination of how connected or addicted we are. The internet and associated technologies grant powerful advantages for making life simpler in many ways, but their abuse results in behaviors harmful to one's mind and way of being in the world.

Growing up with technology doesn't make us more intelligent. It's true that it's facilitated an endless list of activities, but above all it's made it easy to develop a particular mental characteristic: multitasking. Neuroscience refers to this as alternating or divided attention. This means that the brain devotes a few minutes or seconds to carrying out one task, then another, and then another. The brain can't carry out two actions at the same time if they involve the same cerebral area. If we find ourselves listening to song lyrics while reading a book, we aren't carrying out either task to its fullest. An alternation in the focus of our attention arises, because both tasks call on the same area of the brain.

The reality is that, when we multitask, the brain is capable of picking out a lot of information in a superficial way but isn't capable of retaining it. Clifford Nass, a sociologist at Stanford, was one of the pioneers in studying the relationship between attention deficit and multitasking. In spite of what you might think, people who do various things at once—talking on the phone while answering emails, for instance—are less efficient. It's true that they're able to change the focus of their attention with more agility, but studies confirm that this carries with it a memory blockage of the work you've done. If this becomes the norm, we'll end up living in a superficially informed society that in fact lacks real knowledge.

Researchers at the University of Saarland in Germany, Ben Eppinger, Jutta Kray, Barbara Mock, and Axel Mecklinger have published some interesting studies in this area. When the mind alternates between tasks, cerebral circuitry pauses between switching from one to the other, consuming more time and generating less efficiency in the processing of the tasks. We're talking about a reduction of up to 50%!

The twenty-first century is the century of hyperstimulation: thanks (or no thanks) to "new" technologies, the brain is exposed to and obliged to process tremendous quantities of data, which arrive through the senses—mostly sight—erupting in waves or simultaneously. This hyperstimulation has serious consequences; children and young adults, accustomed to this bombardment, require ever stronger and more intense stimulation in order to feel motivated. This undermines their curiosity, sense of wonder, and desire to learn anything that goes beyond the digital world. They find themselves lacking in motivation, and their creativity and imagination are completely undermined. It's not just that—from infancy, they become accustomed to a rhythm of life and an intensity that make serenity and the enjoyment of silence difficult. One could say that children jump constantly from one stimulus to another.

Don't forget that success in life is achieved by people who are capable of concentrating and focusing on what they really want and who are capable of persevering in their goals. The brain's attention is developed in the prefrontal cortex. This area is in charge of volition, self-control, and the planning of tasks. This area of the brain must be developed in children from the time they're small. It is one of the most important areas to be found in the mind.

Let's take a look at how the prefrontal cortex develops, beginning at birth.

A baby begins to pay attention when it sees light; a few months on, its attention focuses on light, movement and sound. The main goal of education consists in getting children to pay attention to things that are neither mobile nor luminous: paper, food, writing, reading, homework, etc. It's a question of channelling their will and attention to make them capable of concentrating voluntarily. If, at this point in their lives, we give children iPads, telephones or tablets, their attention returns to the light-movement-sound stage of development. This isn't an advance for their prefrontal cortex but instead a clear regression, and children are motivated and respond as they did when they were babies. The only difference is that the sounds are more intense, and the lights and movement change at a more vertiginous speed.

Young people's brains need to learn to focus their attention, and to develop the frontal area of the brain—responsible for will and self-control—in a healthy way. An excessive exposure to screens inhibits correct functioning, leading to a clear deficit in attention and concentration. Nowadays there's a lot of emphasis placed on the importance of meditation and mindfulness—paying complete attention. We teach young people not to concentrate and as adults we struggle to recover the capacity for self-control of our minds and attention. There's obviously something we're not doing right.

Hyperconnectivity is intimately related to hyperactivity. ADHD—the well-known attention deficit and hyperactivity disorder—has a strong link to it as well. Young people diagnosed with ADHD have great difficulty with concentration and attention and a low tolerance when faced with frustration. The prolonged use of technology holds out gratifying, easy, attractive alternatives but makes it more difficult to be capable of paying attention to any nondigital stimulus.

We need offline education—above all on an emotional, social level. Face to face communication is the best way to learn how to read others' emotions, as Nass has pointed out. We mustn't forget that our much-discussed emotional intelligence is one of the keys to success in life. The screen is a poor educator when it comes to achieving this. It isolates and insulates the child from everything that surrounds it. It slows the development of the capacity to understand emotions and to connect with other people and their emotions, and it denies the capacity to express what one feels while looking into someone's eyes, rather than at a keyboard or a screen. We must educate children to be capable of savoring life, the emotions, and one-on-one relationships—and for that they must look into our eyes.

Young people connect more easily to a screen, a social network, or a video game than to nature, individuals, and reality. It's not a question of rejecting technology or of denying advances in the digital world but of knowing how to introduce it into the lives of children and adolescents in a sensible, gradual way, teaching them how to exert self-control over their access to apps and online content. We must decide to educate them to connect first with the reality of things, people's emotions, and nature. Having done so, we'll be ready to enter, step by step, into the digital world.

8

HOW TO LOWER CORTISOL LEVELS

EXERCISE

One of the most effective ways to combat stress, anxiety, and depression is to exercise regularly. In this way, you encourage the production of serotonin and dopamine, hormones that reduce anxiety and help combat depression.

> *Careful! Practicing very intense exercise*
> *can raise cortisol levels, because the*
> *body interprets it as a threat.*

In cases of extreme exercise, not only does cortisol not go down, it rises, achieving a peak after 30 to 45 minutes of intense, prolonged exercise, after which it descends little by little to normal levels. The problem is that many times we don't have enough time to get through the barrier where cortisol levels go back down. For this reason, it can be more convenient to carry out gentle, relaxed forms of exercise, like yoga or pilates, or simply walking. A study carried out by biochemist Edward E. Hill, published in 2008 in the *Journal of Endocrinological Investigation*, concluded that exercising at 40 percent intensity was enough to reduce cortisol levels. In addition, if exercise takes place in nature, in the open air, away from the noise and pollution of the big city, it has even more beneficial effects for the body.

The environment in which one practices a sport matters, and quite a bit, too. A study carried out in 2005 by Dr. Jules Pretty, of the biological sciences department at the University of Essex, discovered various psychic benefits to sports practiced in the open air in the countryside—what they called "green exercise"—as opposed to exercise carried out, for example, inside a gym on a city street. The experiment consisted of projecting images on a wall while groups of twenty subjects at a time exercised on treadmills. Four groups ran in front of projections divided into four different categories: pleasant rural images, unpleasant rural images, pleasant urban images, and unpleasant urban images. At the same time, a control group ran without any accompanying projections. They tested the subjects' blood pressure and took note of two aspects of their psychological state (mood and self-esteem) before and after each session. They found that projections of pleasant images, both urban and rural, had a significant positive effect on mood and self-esteem.

Nature and wildlife induce a state of well-being in the majority of people; this is why it's fundamental to mental health to have nearby access to green spaces. Nature helps us to concentrate better, think with greater clarity, and combat mental illnesses that we may have developed.

Merely contemplating nature creates beneficial effects, as Ernest O. Moore demonstrated in 1981, based on the evidence that prisoners who had views of farms in the area surrounding their prisons fell ill less frequently than those whose cells looked into the courtyard of the jail. In a similar vein, Roger S. Ulrich observed in 1984 that patients in a Pennsylvania hospital whose rooms were furnished with windows giving a view of nature required shorter postoperative stays. Contemplating nature is good, but exercise in natural surroundings is better. In a 2014 study published in the journal *Ecopsychology*, Dr. Sara Warber, professor of family medicine in the Medicine School at the University of Michigan, discussed the beneficial effects of walking in a group in the open air: It reduces stress, depression, and negative feelings while increasing positive feelings and mental health.

Exercise helps to direct and balance the hippocampus. When you feel upset, your hippocampus shrinks and the amygdala reacts in a more chaotic way.

In short, moderate exercise carried out in as natural a setting as possible reduces cortisol levels, improves the immune system, and helps us to combat stress, anxiety, and depression.

HANDLING TOXIC PEOPLE

Learn to manage your exposure to those
people who have a toxic effect on you.
Surround yourself with "human vitamins."

Almost all of us have to deal with someone whose mere presence or company—even the simple act of calling them to mind—disrupts our mood.

You probably already know, without having to think too hard, who that person is in your life. Normally the primary cause of this negativity is that, at some point in your trajectory, that person had a perverse influence or a negative impact on your life.

"I feel bad when I'm with him. I'm uncomfortable; he brings out the worst in me. Whatever the subject of conversation, his comments, however subtly, give off some measure of disdain. I don't know if it's all in my head or if there's really something there. I don't know if there's some jealousy or envy . . . Whatever the reason, I feel vulnerable in his presence, and I can only relax and breathe freely when he goes away. Even so, I can't separate myself from him, even though I think I should put some distance between us. This situation is changing my character and creating anguish and sadness in me."

This person might be your partner, your mother, a boss, a colleague, a brother-in-law, a neighbor, a friend. Something about this person's behavior, presence, or way of relating is upsetting, and invariably disturbs your peace.

These are toxic people. There are many kinds: unstable, jealous, paranoid, immature, or neurotic. In each case, they have the ability to destabilize us, sometimes within seconds, offering opinions, gossiping, constantly evaluating our lives, decisions, or comments. They turn themselves into spectators, with the right to offer an opinion on everything we say or do, and, therefore it's very difficult to create healthy bonds with them. At times we're guilty of letting people who we know are like this into our inner circle.

A toxic person becomes a spectator of your life,
with the right to offer an opinion at any time.

They're expert manipulators and they know how to detect the weak points of their victims with absolute precision. A toxic person, by definition, suffocates the people who put up with him. At times it can be intentional; at others, they might not be conscious of the terrible damage they're causing to those around him. Don't confuse a person who is simply going through a bad time and showing a certain temporary irascibility or cynicism with someone who constantly and regularly exerts his toxic effect on anyone who puts up with it.

In principle, toxic people don't bring us anything positive. In the case of a romantic partnership or a family relationship, sometimes a codependent dynamic emerges that can be difficult to see and acknowledge from the inside. We convince ourselves that our inner equilibrium isn't perturbed, and we insist on maintaining the toxic relationship out of a fear of loneliness, which leads us to put up with extreme situations that we shouldn't tolerate.

The key to preventing toxic people from affecting us lies in the attitude we take toward them. We need to make sure that they can't invade our interior world, avoiding, as far as possible, their meddling in our lives, and never allowing them to negate our decision-making capacity. This last barrier, always conserving our freedom to choose, can be impinged on by real or imaginary obstacles that these "emotional vampires" deploy, playing with us in order, very frequently, to break our wills.

Those who let themselves be taken over by toxic personalities may end up with a set of anxious-depressive symptoms, feelings of guilt, dependency, and consequent repercussions for their self-esteem.

SIX KEYS FOR MANAGING A TOXIC PERSON

1. Be discreet with them

At any moment, they might use the information that they have to undermine you or do you harm. People who love you will celebrate your successes and know how to support you in moments of difficulty. Having identified a person who's doing you harm, avoid giving them information about your life.

2. Ignore the opinions of toxic people

In this way, you'll be free, regardless of their remarks and behavior. Have some perspective about what they do—don't give their actions importance. Whether they have influence over you depends on you. Without confronting them directly, learn to put on a "mental raincoat" so that disdainful looks, sarcastic comments, or incisive criticisms roll right off you. You should ask yourself: Do I want this person to have importance in my life?

3. Try to forget about them

Create distance, little by little, or—without being rude—directly. There are people who come into our lives and improve them; and there are others who improve them even more by leaving.

4. If you can't create distance because they're a big part of your life, learn to live with them

If a person is always going to play some part in your life, learn to adapt, and don't make the same mistakes over and over. As time goes by, ask yourself honestly if this person is "globally toxic," creating toxicity and unease with everyone, or "individually toxic," for some reason only having this effect on you.

After this first step, a second stage of analysis consists in uncovering the cause of the toxicity. Try to analyze what's causing you discomfort in your relationship to this person. That is to say, what happens to you when you see them? Do they bring up feelings of inferiority, weakness, rage, fear, anger? Be your own therapist as much as you can, and make use of pen and paper to progress toward a diagnosis. Try to understand the toxic person: What's happening to *them*? Why do they treat me this way?

I've always found it very helpful to remember a phrase already mentioned in this book: understanding is alleviating. In many cases, when we understand the situations that other people are going through, their life stories, their traumas and problems, we can feel compassion for them, and in this way relieve *ourselves* of suffering.

5. Take a risk and forgive

A resentful heart cannot be happy, and many times forgiveness is the best cure that exists. If a vehicle carries out a dangerous or aggressive maneuver, we might think the driver is a lunatic, and start honking and insulting him—something that won't give us peace, but will increase our cortisol levels—or we can see him as someone anxious and unhappy, feel compassion, and forgive.

6. Keep your "human vitamins" close

These people produce the contrary effect to toxic people in our bodies and brains. They're capable of bringing joy to our hearts within seconds. I recommend keeping good, joyful people within reach, people who have healthy intentions, who activate and enrich your inner equilibrium. "Human vitamins" are those people who always seem able to remind us of the joy of living. We need to spend as much time with them as possible.

Misery loves company, and bitterness is contagious.
If you're at a vulnerable point, referring back
to a person like that might sink you and bring
out your worst qualities. When you stop feeling
vulnerable around toxic people, you'll have won
an important battle in the war for happiness.

POSITIVE THOUGHTS

Throughout this book, we've been discussing the importance of training your thoughts. Now let's look at some concrete guidelines for reining in the cascade of negative thoughts and stopping or redirecting the torrent of worries that engulfs us each day.

Enjoying life requires us to be capable of having perspective about its negative aspects and of knowing how to take pleasure in the little things. Living in a constant state of high alert, distress, or sadness prevents us from finding the peace and balance necessary to happiness. The majority of the things that worry us are an accumulation of "microworries" that, added together, disturb our inner world.

To avoid worries, we need to substitute constructive, positive occupations and ideas for anxious ones. Occupy yourself with plans, hobbies, people . . . whatever it takes to get out of the toxic cycle in which we all unconsciously trap ourselves sometimes. I love this saying, attributed to Van Gogh: "If you hear a voice within you say 'you cannot paint,' then by all means paint, and that voice will be silenced."

There is an inner voice I like to call the "thought commentator." This is that voice that comments on every throw in the game, on your environment, and the people you encounter. It is intimately related to your personal judgments, internal criticisms, and frustrations. Teaching this voice helps you to recover equilibrium. In psychotherapy, I work a lot on this issue: finding a way to slow down the devastating current of negative thoughts that engulf and block us.

> *Negative thoughts have a toxic impact, whose effects can last in the body for several hours. Living stuck in a recurrent toxic thought is distressing and disrupts the optimal functioning of the body.*

A SIMPLE GUIDE TO WORRYING LESS

The basis for these ideas is the notion that we can restructure the brain and the automatisms that arise in the mind, blocking you each time you recur to them. You should be aware that your thoughts are real. They exist. Even though you can't touch them or hear them out loud, they have strength and the capacity to change you.

- Is the thing that's worrying me significant, or does it lack importance? Pause for a moment: could it be that my mind is tricking me, magnifying or distorting this issue? Accept that thoughts don't always tell the truth. Sometimes they're correct, but in many other cases they falsify reality.
- What emotion is coming up for me? Keeping in mind our schema of reality, what is my mood today? What's the possible cause of this dip or moment of vulnerability? Sleep, drugs, tiredness, external circumstances?
- Observe the impact that every negative thought has on your body. Become aware of how a toxic or harmful thought can influence you physically (tachycardia, sweating, headache, gastrointestinal discomfort, muscle tightness, etc.)
- Don't automatically translate every thought into words. We are the lords of our silence and the slaves of our speech. Pause and reflect on

what you're going to say, and the consequences it will have, before you express yourself.

- Have I been able to successfully deal with what's worrying me, or with a similar issue, at another point in my life? What was the first step for getting out of the locked groove?

- Don't assume you know what other people are thinking: "I'm sure that they think this about me ..." Your suspicions might be unfounded. Don't prejudge.

- Speak kindly to yourself. Say something about yourself that is true and that helps you to feel more secure.

- Feel the positive emotion, allowing it to bring you a sense of physical well-being.

- Anchor yourself in the present and focus on your ability to act in the here and now.

- Have a vision of the future. Decide if this battle is worth waging. Get perspective. Ask yourself if what seems essential now will have so much importance in a year.

- Don't act or respond if you have automatic negative thoughts. Wait and give yourself a chance. Be capable of changing your language, for example, by replacing the word "problem" with "challenge," or "mistake" with "second chance." Employ words that exude optimism, like "joy," "peace," "hope," "trust," "passion," or "excitement."

- Look for the positive in every situation. Every situation can be looked at from an angle that emphasizes either problems or solutions. Think of Thomas Edison's remark, "I have not failed. I've just found 10,000 ways that won't work."

- A little piece of advice for when you're stuck in a thought loop: Write the whirlwind of your thoughts down on a piece of paper and refute them. For example: "My sister-in-law hates me." Give that thought a reply: "She's having a bad day; she's not usually this hard on me." You might be tricking yourself, but in the end, practicing this simple exercise will have healthy consequences for your body and mind.

Your inner voice should support you, not undermine you. Be careful not to get in your own way—you may make yourself fail even before you've started.

MEDITATION/MINDFULNESS

In the depths of every human being, there are powerful sources of healing whose mechanisms are still unknown. I'm referring to healthy introspection, meditation, and prayer. The mind, thanks to these processes, can act on the body and restore it. Here I'm going to offer a simple sketch of this discipline.

What Is Mindfulness?

Mindfulness means complete attention to the present moment. It is the art of intentionally and attentively observing our consciousness. It's a concept drawn from Buddhist meditation. The core of mindfulness is attending exclusively to the here and now.

Practicing it in Western society is no simple matter; it can be truly counterintuitive, and requires an open mind. It invokes our spiritual dimension and at times transcends the logic that generally guides our lives. However, mindfulness is not religion in disguise. At its base, there's nothing mystical or magical about it; it's simply common sense. It only requires a mental examination, with the aim of discovering what is making your mind ill and what can cure it. In recent decades, scientific studies on this practice have multiplied revealing the benefits to body and mind that meditation and mindfulness in particular can confer.

The supernatural or spiritual dimension of a human being has an extraordinary power over both mind and body. Among people who live out their faith—whatever form it takes—with fidelity and peace, this translates, according to some studies, into lower stress. This is due to multiple factors, but we can intuit that having a sense of meaning in one's life, a supportive community, goals, and purpose accompanied by prayer or meditation as a mechanism for grappling with problems and difficulties, contributes to that longed-for sense of inner peace.

A few years ago I was working in London, in the psychiatry department of King's College. I was collaborating with and learning from Professor Andrea Danese, a researcher who was, at that time, in the midst of investigating the relationship between meditation and physical health, specifically inflammation. I remember asking him one day, while eating lunch in the hospital cafeteria, if the effects were similar across Buddhist meditation, mindfulness, and Christian or Jewish prayer. His response was clear: yes, as long as the practice is carried out under conditions of acceptance and surrender. He explained that the problem with prayer and some meditation techniques is that the individual comes to the practice requesting, demanding, imploring . . . in short, in a state of anguish, which, rather than alleviating their distress, creates more of it.

Investing a little time in meditating with complete attention on what our senses are experiencing in the present moment helps us gain time, increasing the efficiency of everything we undertake, improving our attention and concentration, our ability to learn new things, and our creativity. Practicing mindfulness exercises the brain in the same way that practicing a sport exercises the muscles.

Prayer adds another fundamental layer. In the case of mindfulness, the key resides in releasing negative thoughts together with achieving a full awareness of the senses and the here and now. When a spiritual vision of existence is also present, as in prayer, faith in a superior being is added to the benefits of mindfulness, along with an intimate trust that everything that happens to us has meaning.

The belief system associated with most religions emphasizes caring for personal relationships, promulgating empathy in an active way, and cultivating love for others and the capacity to forgive.

Mindfulness and Business

The world of business currently gives enormous importance to mindfulness, given that it has been demonstrated that the benefit of multitasking is nothing more than a myth, and that carrying out various activities at a time has an associated decrease in efficiency. When we undertake various tasks simultaneously, we invest a lot more time, commit more errors, and struggle more to remember things related to our work. On the other hand, when we are totally present and intent on our work, our labor is more efficient, we make more confident decisions, and we collaborate more effectively with colleagues.

Studies have also been carried out exploring the effectiveness of mindfulness practice in the world of business. In 1979, working with the medical center of the University of Massachusetts, the New Yorker Jon Kabat-Zinn developed a program called Mindfulness-Based Stress Reduction, lasting eight weeks. The results were conclusive: stress levels had gone down and participants felt they had more energy at work. Furthermore, they observed that activity in the left prefrontal area of the brain—which regulates the activation of the amygdala and stimulates the parasympathetic nervous system—had increased, and participants presented a greater production of antibodies when exposed to a flu virus than a control group that hadn't participated in the mindfulness course.

This practice is playing an ever-greater role in businesses around the world. The benefits are obvious.

Mindfulness and the Immune System

In recent years, Dr. David S. Black, assistant professor of preventative medicine at the Keck School of Medicine at the University of Southern California, has published numerous studies on the health benefits of mindfulness. He carried out the first exhaustive survey of randomly controlled testing that examined the effects of mindfulness on five parameters of the immune system: stimulation and circulation of inflammatory proteins, genetic expression and cellular transcription factors, quantity of immune cells, the aging of these cells, and antibody response. His findings suggested interesting effects from mindfulness: a significant reduction in the specific markers of inflammation (whose harmful effects we know well!), a high number of CD4 T lymphocytes—these are like the "generals" of the immune system—and increased telomerase activity, resulting in an elongation of the telomeres.[*] These studies are just the beginning, but the results are encouraging.

> *Be proactive. Don't be afraid to believe in the transcendent meaning of your being and your life. First, learn to breathe with attention in moments of calm, when you aren't stressed or in crisis. Train your mind little by little, gradually. Pay attention to what's around you, while also connecting in a deep way with your essence; you'll discover a wonderful world.*

OMEGA-3

All of my patients, family members, and random people who happen to cross my path in life know that I'm an enthusiastic proponent of omega-3 supplements. It all began a few years ago. I started suffering a severe problem with my gums, and a dietician friend recommended that I start taking omega-3 every day. Much to my surprise, after a few weeks, my problems cleared up all at once. I've observed that after periods of intense stress, this discomfort returns, but fish oil halts its harmful effects.

Ingesting omega-3 is a very healthy way of boosting your mood and

---

[*] Remember that telomere length acts as a measure of the number of times a cell can divide, and therefore of our remaining lifespan.

cognitive capacities. Although there are six types of omega-3 fatty acids, only three of them connect to human physiology: α-Linolenic acid (ALA), eicosapentaenoic acid (EPA), and docosahexaenoic acid (DHA). We'll concentrate on the last two.

They're usually referred to as essential fatty acids because they have vital importance for certain bodily functions and because none of these fatty acids can be produced autonomously inside the body, which is why it's necessary to include them in the diet.

EPA (eicosapentaenoic acid) is the precursor of certain eicosanoids. These are lipid molecules—fats—that perform certain important anti-inflammatory and immune functions. This fatty acid can be obtained by ingesting fish (salmon, sardines, tuna, mackerel, herring) and fish oil (cod liver oil). In internal medicine, this fatty acid is employed as a lipid-lowering medication—it lowers levels of cholesterol and triglycerides in the blood.

DHA (docosahexaenoic acid) is principally found in fish oil as well, but also in certain algae, like spirulina. In reality, these algae are its origin point—fish feed on the algae, and little by little it concentrates inside them, working its way up the food chain. It's particularly concentrated in the brain, retinas, and reproductive cells. Neurons and the gray matter of the brain are composed mostly of fat, which is why this component is key for their development and correct functioning. The brain requires an adequate level of DHA for optimal development. Where this is not the case, we're faced with a deficit in neurogenesis and the metabolism of neurotransmitters.

Omega-3 has an important anti-inflammatory function.

Studies carried out by the American nutritional biochemist William E. M. Lands since 2005 have demonstrated that excess levels of omega-6 in relation to the omega-3 levels are associated with heart attacks, arthritis, osteoporosis, depression and mood swings, obesity, and cancer. An excess of omega-6 forms the basis for multiple pathologies. In 2002, the Greek-born doctor Artemis P. Simopoulos published evidence that not only is it important to ingest essential fatty acids, it is even more crucial to maintain a healthy proportion of omega-6 to omega-3. We humans have evolved consuming them in a 1:1 ratio, but in recent decades, due to the rise in meat consumption and processed foods, this proportion has risen to 10:1 in Western diets—in the United States it can even rise to 30:1. It has been demonstrated that diminishing the amount of omega-6 can help to prevent cardiovascular diseases, asthma, rheumatoid arthritis, and colorectal cancer.

Breast milk contains DHA—as long as the mother has ingested it beforehand—and it is vital to the neural and cerebral development of nursing babies; mothers are also advised to ingest this fatty acid during the gestation period. But DHA isn't only vital during infancy; studies are beginning to emerge that link adequate levels of omega-3 to a significant decrease in the likelihood of developing dementia or Alzheimer's. Conversely, low DHA levels in old age have been associated with a rise in the probability of accelerated cognitive decline. The brain is deeply dependent on this fatty acid, and low levels have been related to depression, cognitive deterioration, and other disorders. Patients with memory deficits, after ingesting one gram of DHA daily for six months, have experienced an improvement in their memories. In addition, patients diagnosed with Alzheimer's, after ingesting omega-3 supplements, have experienced a slower development of the disease. DHA is also pointed to as a principal source of neuroprotectin, a substance implicated in the survival and repair of brain cells.

Taking fish oil every day has healthy and beneficial effects at multiple levels. A positive correlation has even been observed, in a study published in 2010 by Dr. Afshin Farzaneh-Far of the University of Illinois, between high omega-3 levels and telomere length.

Finally, the benefits of fish oil include an improvement in attentive capacity and ADHD symptoms. Young people who ingest omega-3 show an improvement in test scores. Today, the American Psychiatric Association—and many manuals of mental health—recommend ingesting omega-3 as a preventative measure to slow or halt the development of certain mental illnesses, such as schizophrenia, depression, and bipolar disorder; it has also been recommended as part of their treatment of these illnesses.

I recommend taking one or two grams of omega-3 daily. There are multiple studies that attest the beneficial effects—both anti-depressive and anti-inflammatory—of this complex.

9

BEST POSSIBLE SELF

To achieve any kind of success or triumph in life, one must begin here, with a process that might at first seem simple, but which isn't easy to carry out correctly.

WHO AM I?

Knowing oneself is the first step in overcoming oneself. To initiate an internal process of self-overcoming and transformation, I usually follow these three steps with my patients, and I recommend that you do the same:

1. **Know myself**

   I need to know what I am like. What characterizes me? What do I like the most about myself, or the least? I always say there are four facets to the process of gaining self-knowledge:
   - What others perceive about me: my image
   - What I believe I am: my self-conception

- What I truly am: my essence
- What I show on online platforms: my *digital* image

2. Understand myself

This means knowing what has led me to respond as I do when faced with certain situations, understanding my genes, my past, my way of relating to others (bosses, friends, employees, partners). Recall your childhood carefully. Avoid impossible therapies where you end up pitted against your origins! When you're conscious of your limitations, barriers, and fears, and you understand where they come from, you're making huge steps forward in your inner work and expanding your capacity to manage your emotions.

3. Accept myself

Assimilating certain things that are the way they are, and can't be modified, whatever I do. It's important to accept that we have limitations, make mistakes, and can be wrong. Succeeding in life doesn't come from being flawless and making no mistakes, but from learning to make the most of our abilities and aptitudes.

There's no reason your flaws should hold you back, as long as you're aware of them and know how to balance them out with your strengths.

Life's winners are those people who enjoy their work and are really excellent at something in particular. They're no different than you, it's just that they've devoted their time to polishing and refining their abilities and to trying to make the most of them by focusing on something that they're good at or that they love. We don't all have the luck to work in a field that excites us, but a happy, successful person, a professional capable of leading the way, loves what they do and does it well. As an old book says, "Love your work, and grow old in it."

Talent + Passion = Vocation

If you call to mind people that you deeply admire, it doesn't matter what field they work in—they could be athletes, entrepreneurs, journalists, doctors, spiritual leaders, writers—you'll notice that all of them are individuals who picked one thing to concentrate on, and strengthened their abilities in that area. I don't mean they can't play well in many keys, as it were, but they know how to focus on a particular thing that they do better than other people. Any person that you bring to mind right now—really anyone!—has some degree of inner conflict and has suffered to get to where they are.

I remember at a conference a few years ago, I met a very famous singer. He had sold millions of albums and performed at packed concerts all over the world. Something about him, beyond his music, inspired me and came across when I met him. I was a real "fangirl," and I came up to him to ask if I could take a photo. He was someone who, one to one, showed a surprising amount of warmth and attention, asking me about my family and my job. When I said I was a psychiatrist, he told me, "I've been in therapy for a long time. I have panic attacks in crowded places, and sometimes even on stage. It's my daily struggle. I hope to overcome it completely one day."

A world-famous singer who panics in crowded places! I've seen concerts of his on YouTube and in person; I've never forgotten that brief conversation, and it makes me smile to think that, in spite of his debilitating fear, this man triumphs wherever he appears.

ROGER FEDERER

Federer is a living legend, without a doubt the best and most elegant male tennis player in history. He's broken all the records in his sport and has fans all over the world. In an interview published in July 2013 in the paper *Marca*, his interviewer said, "You've always had a great serve, a better forehand, an excellent volley, as well as variety in your slide. Your weak point seems to be the backhand."

"I had two options," Federer replied, "make the most of my strengths or improve my weaknesses. If I did the second, I would become a more predictable tennis player. In the end, my virtues are what pays the bills. I can't see myself doing what lots of people do and hitting a thousand balls with a backhand to try and get better."

So, what *is* a leader? A leader needs three qualities: a message, the ability to communicate it, and optimism about the results.

It's difficult at the moment to find anyone who inspires in this way. The politicians who occupy the airwaves often don't know how to communicate, and normally their messages are ambiguous and calculated, changing according to the public they're addressing or want to seduce. "Leaders" like that aren't worth anything. The people who make a mark, who can bring the rest of us along with them, are the ones who radiate coherence, peace, and happiness.

BPS: BEST POSSIBLE SELF

A successful life requires reflection, knowledge, work, effort, a sense of humor . . . it's quite a list! I've formulated an equation that, to me, expresses how to achieve your BPS for life.

Your BPS requires, above all, a zest for life! This means that, despite life's twists and turns, you always make the effort to be the best that you can. This obviously can't be learned in a book—it's learned by living, enjoying, feeling, and relishing your life, but above all by falling down and getting up again.

You are the result of your own decisions. You must realize that your decisions condition your life, and you can't just let yourself be swept along.

BPS = (Knowledge + Willpower + Life goals) x Passion

I've said that you're the result of your decisions; with enough passion, and by exerting and strengthening your willpower, you can achieve almost anything you want. I say "almost" because there's another factor—you can call it luck, destiny, or providence—that may not always let you triumph or achieve your goals, however realistic they are. But first, let's look at the risks.

It's like any equation:

- If you're lacking knowledge . . . there's nothing more dangerous than a passionate, motivated fool!
- If you're lacking willpower . . . you'll start off full of knowledge and excitement, but this will fade quickly!
- If you're lacking a life goal . . . you'll be a slave of immediacy, in thrall to instant gratification!
- If you're lacking passion . . . you'll never be a leader, you'll never shine, and you'll spoil the other elements of the formula—plus you won't enjoy the benefits of passion that lead to a healthy old age!

KNOWLEDGE

> *Chance only favors the prepared mind.*
>
> —Louis Pasteur

This quotation from the French scientist always encourages me. Later, the writer Isaac Asimov reiterated this thought, explaining that only he who prepares, studies, and exerts himself with vigor and will can aspire to success in life.

This idea, applied to the questions that concern us here, possesses enormous force. Maybe chance—or providence!—will come to meet us, but we won't be able to see it or take advantage of it in the right way. Fortune favors the prepared and educated person, one who has acquired skills and knowledge sufficient to seize luck when it arrives . . . if it arrives. We are all in possession of a powerful tool for achieving our goals: Our capacity to study and cultivate ourselves. The question is, are you ready to learn?

In treatment, we often apply "bibliotherapy." We recommend books on psychology and self-improvement at a certain level, to help patients understand what's happening to them or provide guidelines for overcoming it; and alongside these, we recommend novels that suck them in or help them find a way out of negative thoughts or toxic emotional states.

Avoid the idiot box, hours lost online, and YouTube. Go outside, exercise, read—these are powerful antidepressants and anxiolytics.

WILLPOWER

Don't forget that your best possible self emerges when you focus on your abilities, working hard on them in an ordered, disciplined, consistent way. You have to learn to give everything you have, every day of your life … according to the abilities you've got.

What Is Willpower?

Willpower is the ability to postpone gratification and reward. A person with willpower has a long view of life, and is capable of setting concrete goals and taking risks to achieve them. Willpower requires determination, decision, and stamina.

The difference between wanting and desiring is rooted in willpower. Wanting requires making a firm decision. Desire seeks possession or gratification of the instant variety: food, drink, sex, or some other impulse. It has a speed component and fulfills a person momentarily but doesn't enhance them. On the other hand, "wanting" seeks a further goal, which requires a concrete, well-designed plan, and putting continual effort in to achieve it. It's a fuller process, because it helps us to grow as human beings.

Having a well-trained will is the result of continual personal work sustained by effort and sacrifice, which transforms us into strong, consistent people, capable of seeking not what's easiest, but what is *best* for each of us. It isn't genetic, but acquired; you aren't born with it, but you can conquer it.

Willpower is determination. It's choosing a specific direction, having previously reflected on it, evaluating the pros and cons and proceeding toward your goal. One of the clearest indicators of a mature personality is having a strong will. And the reverse is true too: one of the most obvious symptoms of an immature personality is having a weak, fragile, breakable will, which quickly abandons the struggle to reach a proposed goal.

This section could be expanded to fill an entire book (and such books do exist). Order, constancy, perseverance, and effort are the motors that propel any project or enterprise forward. Without them, however good your ideas are, they'll end up getting watered down and losing their force.

Having a well-trained will helps us to move
toward the best version of our life goals.

SETTING GOALS AND OBJECTIVES

Goals are long-term, objectives short-term. Seneca the Younger said, "There is no favorable wind for the sailor who doesn't know where to go." A person who doesn't have a plan is at the mercy of the moment. He reacts according to impulses, emotions, or feelings, all of which—especially in our society—are extremely malleable.

There are always people who have begun their projects in worse circumstances than yours, but they've gotten where they wanted to go. Don't be afraid to change your goals and objectives if it's necessary to do so for your physical or mental health, or to improve your relationship with your partner, family, or friends. The habits and customs that have built up around your way of being have a huge influence on your life. People make the decision to create true change during serious crises, whether personal, financial, familial, or medical. As Dr. Valentín Fuster, cardiologist at Mount

Sinai in New York, has aptly said: "The best way to stop smoking is to have a heart attack."

Let your heart soar, sketch out a plan
of action, and execute it.

One's life project emerges from having a focus to hang on to and use for support. Have a plan, be realistic, and go out and find it. I said at the beginning of the book that few sentiments have done as much damage as the phrase, "It will come when you least expect it." This idea draws us into a passive, waiting attitude, which is very dangerous—"it" might never come. Don't be afraid to get excited, imagine something great, make a plan, and carry it out! Having a plan carries with it the personal satisfaction of being able to relish the different achievements or milestones you reach. In those small steps you take lies the root of true happiness—not in obsessing over a goal! It's fundamental to know how to revise your plans according to circumstances, or else you might end up profoundly frustrated by failure.

PASSION

We should spend more time on what makes
us truly happy.

—Anonymous

Passion doesn't add—it multiplies. It improves neural connections, fortifies neurogenesis—the production of new neurons—and lengthens telomeres. We are created to be happy, transmit that happiness to others, and share the good things in life. An interesting fact: According to studies carried out at the Mayo Clinic, life expectancy in pessimists is reduced by up to 19 percent.

What did Pep Guardiola say when he started coaching at Barcelona? "I give you my word that we'll try our hardest. I don't know if we'll win or lose, but we'll try. Fasten your seat belts. We're gonna have a good time." And it

was true; for years we—even Real Madrid fans!—got to enjoy some spec-
tacular football.

Can you learn to be an optimist?

Absolutely, you can. Israeli psychologist Tal Ben-Shahar leads the most
popular course at Harvard University, which teaches you how to be happy.
We can learn to be positive. It's a slow job, but one that's full of satisfaction
and opportunities to improve our physical and mental health. Optimism is
a way of holding on to the present moment, even though, as I've emphasized
over the course of this book, happiness isn't what happens to us, but how we
interpret what happens. The people who have gone furthest in life had an
optimistic vision of the world and others and knew how to communicate
it to those around them. An optimist knows how to see their goals, while a
pessimist always finds an excuse not to go after them.

> *As Murray Butler aptly said, there are three kinds of*
> *people in the world: those who make things happen,*
> *those who watch things happen, and those who never*
> *know what happened. What kind of person are you?*

IT'S NEVER TOO LATE
TO START AGAIN

The Case of Judith, the Porn Star

I met Judith at the end of a lecture on education and resilience I gave at a college. She came up to speak to me and said, "I'm an actress. I saw online that you were giving a talk at this college, and I decided to come. I don't want to keep living. I can't do it anymore. I'm going to kill myself."

I was completely frozen. I don't know much about film, much less international cinema (she had a light foreign accent). I asked her name, and just at that moment, the director of the college came up to present me with a book published in honor of the institution's 50th anniversary. I took advantage of the interruption to look her up on Google. She was a porn actress, with more than a million online followers!

I turned back to her and asked her about the cause of her sadness. She explained that her long-time boyfriend—they had known each other since childhood—had asked her to marry him. She loved him, though she had a few doubts ("I'm not sure I'm in love . . . or if I'm even capable of falling in love!"), but she knew she didn't have a future with him. She told me, "He wants me to stop acting, and I'm ready to do it, but if we have children ... you can't understand ... if they looked me up online one day ... I don't have a future."

Very delicately, still standing by the stage where I had given my talk, we began to touch on the subject of pornography. I referred to it very carefully, to avoid hurting her, and she noticed what I was doing.

"Thank you for not judging me. I need help ... What worries me most is not being able to erase my past, heal my wounds, and begin again."

I fixed an appointment for early the following morning with her. I spent the whole night turning the issue over and over in my mind—and then I called an acquaintance who works in law enforcement to ask what's required for someone to change their identity.

The next morning I had all the necessary information. Her mother was foreign and her father was Spanish, so she had dual nationality. We spoke about the possibility of changing her name, even though she already used a pseudonym for her work. We cautiously began to explore her past, discussing how she had ended up shooting in different countries, occasionally intersecting with the world of high-end prostitution and drug-dealing. She had many deep wounds that needed healing.

She slowly revealed more of her life story to me. Very carefully, we dove into her childhood, her mother's abandonment of her, her father's alcoholism and later suicide. At the age of 10 she suffered sexual abuse at the hands of a close relative. At 18, then a beautiful adolescent, she began to attract boys. That was when she met Raúl, her long-time boyfriend. She didn't want anything serious, but he declared his undying love for her the first day they met and promised to wait as long as she needed.

Soon, she was offered work as a model in a foreign country, and she accepted. She needed money. At night she went partying, and that was where she entered into contact with the world of drugs and high-end prostitution, both of which paid very well. She stopped feeling anything. She faked everything. Every night she wept without tears, lost in an internal void that did nothing but grow. Raúl, who knew her situation, looked for her and tried to get her out of that world, but without success. He gave her books and sent her recordings of lectures, so that she would hear people talk about overcoming pain and trauma.

After a few weeks of therapy, she was much calmer. She was undertaking all the steps necessary to change her life and appearance. She didn't have a particularly distinctive face, and with a little bit of effort she was able to alter her look.

A few months after I met her, she brought Raúl to a session. He was a profoundly good man, who had always loved her and knew that she had enormous potential, which had been damaged by the life she was leading.

A few months ago, I received this letter:

Dear Doctor,

I've just arrived in my new country. It's not really new—my mother grew up a hundred kilometers away from where we've set up house. I've started a clothing business, which is going slowly, but I'm very excited about it. I have my savings, and, if all goes well, we'll get married next spring. I've found my desire to live again, so thank you for your help! [. . .]

It's never too late to start again.

P.S. I sent your details to some of the girls I used to work with so that you can help them too. Don't tell them where I am.

Yours affectionately,
Judith

AUTHOR'S NOTE TO THE 10TH SPANISH EDITION

Dear Reader,

Medicine in general, and psychiatry in particular, are very vocational professions. Ever since I was a girl, I felt a desire to help others and dedicate my life to the training that would allow me to do so. The book that you have between your hands is the result of many years of study, dozens of articles read, hundreds or perhaps thousands of patients treated with care, common sense, and a continuous willingness to learn.

The positive reception that has greeted this book gives me special joy. I'm convinced that every person who has held this book in their hands had one purpose, whether they were conscious of it or not: to know themselves. "Know thyself"—this same phrase was written on the temple of Apollo at Delphi, the epicenter of Greek civilization, and one of the roots of Western civilization. Understanding ourselves, comprehending why what happens to us happens, is a titanic undertaking, but it's also the first step to achieving inner peace and strengthening our relationship to those around us.

Since the publication of this book, I've received many messages from readers that are pleased with having made progress in the difficult work of knowing themselves, which has led them to improve their lives. Thanks to this book and to my readers—thanks to you—I've discovered another way of putting into practice my vocation of helping others.

I hope that this book, more than merely being enjoyable to read, is useful to you in your life—and may good things happen to you!

ACKNOWLEDGMENTS

My first thanks, without a doubt, go to Jesús, for his unconditional and untiring support. Without him I would never have been able to write this book. To Jesusín, for his endless joy; to Enrique, for bringing out my strength when I was at my weakest; to Javier, for accompanying me from the first page to the last.

To my father, for being my teacher and guide in the science of the soul.

To my mother, for showing me that with effort and passion, anything can be achieved.

To Cristina, for her loyalty and companionship throughout my life.

To Isabel, for walking hand in hand with me through the world of emotions and in this exciting profession of helping others.

To the doctors and professors who have trained me over the years.

To my patients, true teachers, for allowing me to play a part in their lives during difficult moments and for bringing me joy through their recovery.

To Planeta and Espasa for giving me the opportunity to pour into a book everything I wanted to communicate.

To Fernando, for his patience in correcting the original text.

Finally, I want to give thanks to Almudena and Quique, united to a higher power, for watching over me and being by my side every day.

BIBLIOGRAPHY

Amen, Daniel. *Change Your Brain, Change Your Life.* St Louis, MO: Turtleback, 2015.

American Psychiatric Association. *DSM-5: Diagnostic and Statistical Manual of Mental Disorders.* Washington, DC: APA Publishing, 2013.

Aron, Elaine. *The Highly Sensitive Person.* New York: Birch Lane Press, 1996.

Ben-Shahar, Tal. *Being Happy: You Don't Have to Be Perfect to Lead a Richer, Happier Life.* New York: McGraw-Hill, 2010.

Bullmore, Edward. *The Inflamed Mind: A Radical New Approach to Depression.* London: Shortbooks, 2018.

Carnegie, Dale. *How to Win Friends & Influence People.* New York: Simon & Schuster, 2011.

Carr, Nicholas G. "Is Google Making Us Stupid?" *The Atlantic,* July-August 2008.

Cyrulnik, Boris. *Resilience: How Your Inner Strength Can Set You Free From the Past.* New York: Tarcher, 2011.

Dyer, Wayne. *Your Erroneous Zones.* New York: HarperPerennial, 2001.

Frankl, Viktor. *Man's Search for Meaning.* London: Rider, 2004.

Goleman, Daniel. *Emotional Intelligence: Why It Can Matter More Than IQ.* New York: Bantam Books, 1996.

L'Ecuyer, Catherine. *The Wonder Approach.* London: Robinson, 2019.

Mam, Somaly. *The Road of Lost Innocence.* London: Virago, 2009.

Pert, Candace. *Molecules of Emotion.* New York: Scribner, 2012.

Puig, Mario. *Reinventing Yourself.* Singapore: Marshall Cavendish, 2011.

Rotella, Bob. *How Champions Think.* New York: Simon & Schuster, 2015.

Seligman, Martin. *Learned Optimism: How to Change Your Mind and Your Life.* London: Nicholas Brealey Publishing, 2018.

Sonnenfeld, Alfred. *How to Raise an Adult.* Scotts Valley, CA: CreateSpace, 2017.

Tolle, Eckhart. *Practising the Power of Now.* London: Yellow Kite, 2016.

Wiesenthal, Simon. *The Sunflower: On the Possibilities and Limits of Forgiveness.* New York: Schocken Books, 1998.

INDEX